# THE
# Good Life
# for Less

# THE
# Good Life
# for Less

Giving Your Family Great Meals,
Good Times, and a
Happy Home on a Budget

## AMY ALLEN CLARK

with Jana Murphy

A PERIGEE BOOK

**A PERIGEE BOOK**
**Published by the Penguin Group**
**Penguin Group (USA) Inc.**
**375 Hudson Street, New York, New York 10014, USA**
Penguin Group (Canada), 90 Eglinton Avenue East, Suite 700, Toronto, Ontario M4P 2Y3, Canada
(a division of Pearson Penguin Canada Inc.) • Penguin Books Ltd., 80 Strand, London WC2R 0RL,
England • Penguin Ireland, 25 St. Stephen's Green, Dublin 2, Ireland (a division of Penguin
Books Ltd.) • Penguin Group (Australia), 707 Collins Street, Melbourne, Victoria 3008, Australia
(a division of Pearson Australia Group Pty Ltd.) • Penguin Books India Pvt. Ltd., 11 Community
Centre, Panchsheel Park, New Delhi—110 017, India • Penguin Group (NZ), 67 Apollo Drive,
Rosedale, Auckland 0632, New Zealand (a division of Pearson New Zealand Ltd.) • Penguin Books,
Rosebank Office Park, 181 Jan Smuts Avenue, Parktown North 2193, South Africa • Penguin China,
B7 Jaiming Center, 27 East Third Ring Road North, Chaoyang District, Beijing 100020, China
Penguin Books Ltd., Registered Offices: 80 Strand, London WC2R 0RL, England

While the author has made every effort to provide accurate telephone numbers, Internet addresses, and
other contact information at the time of publication, neither the publisher nor the author assumes any
responsibility for errors, or for changes that occur after publication. Further, the publisher does not have
any control over and does not assume any responsibility for author or third-party websites or their content.

THE GOOD LIFE FOR LESS

First edition: January 2013

ISBN: 978-0-399-16029-5

An application to catalog this book has been submitted to the Library of Congress.

PRINTED IN THE UNITED STATES OF AMERICA

10  9  8  7  6  5  4  3  2  1

The recipes contained in this book are to be followed exactly as written. The publisher is not
responsible for your specific health or allergy needs that may require medical supervision. The
publisher is not responsible for any adverse reactions to the recipes contained in this book.

Most Perigee books are available at special quantity discounts for bulk purchases
for sales promotions, premiums, fund-raising, or educational use. Special books, or book
excerpts, can also be created to fit specific needs. For details, write: Special Markets,
Penguin Group (USA) Inc., 375 Hudson Street, New York, New York 10014.

*Dedicated to Ethan & Emily*

*My inspiration for all the good things in life.*

# CONTENTS

# INTRODUCTION

Some of us learn to budget and live frugally while we're still banking out of a ceramic pig with a coin slot in its back. Personally, I didn't start figuring it out until I was grown and married, nine months pregnant, and facing looming financial ruin. I was working as an insurance agent, and my husband had a promising job at a dot-com start-up. We were making great money and living a life that seems luxurious to me now. We ate out often and spent money freely. We weren't reckless, though; we were saving as much as we could. Still, we were counting on things to remain the same, and that wasn't meant to be.

We had decided I would stay home with our son after his birth, and I was counting the days until I'd become a first-time—and full-time—mom. I vividly remember my husband's midday appearance at my office, and the sinking feeling in my heart when

I looked at his face. We sat on a bench just outside the office as he broke the news to me that he had been laid off—a blow neither of us ever saw coming. Everything in our world was about to change.

Shocked, and days away from becoming first-time parents, we examined our finances and went into emergency mode. Not only would I not be a stay-at-home mom but my job suddenly became the only source of income we had. Our first real, carefully made budget was one in which no matter how we looked at it, our income was not going to cover our bills. It was too late to start spending carefully, or to put aside money for tough times. We were in big trouble, and we were going to be there for a few years to come.

If I could go back and whisper in my own ear when I was a newlywed, I would tell her to be careful with money—to live frugally from the beginning, to not waste, and to be grateful for all the true blessings in her life: a happy marriage, good health, a roof over her head, and the precious family we were about to start. I'd tell her that even though the happy couple might one day prove you actually *can* live on love for a year or two, it's a lot easier to both live and love if you have enough money to pay the bills.

With a little luck and a lot of pluck, Ryan and I were able to get back on solid financial ground, a journey I documented on my website, MomAdvice.com. I learned to embrace living small and spending carefully, and I discovered that I find great happiness in knowing we live a life we can sustain—even if misfortune ever comes calling again.

This book is the handbook that I wish I'd had when I was just beginning to learn how to make the most of our money. It starts with the basics of establishing a budget and walks you through getting the most for your dollar, whether you're shopping for groceries or paying the electric bill. Equally important, it shares countless ways to ensure that even while you are living frugally, you are living well—creating family traditions, foods, and celebrations that the people you love will cherish and remember. This is not a book about "doing without." It's a book about making the most of your money; spending carefully and wisely; and using your wits, creativity, and goodwill to give your family a good life for less.

Fortunately for me, frugal habits have become a way of life for our family. My husband and I now have two beautiful children, a home of our own, and careers that seem to be on the upswing. But I have become, for life, a penny-pincher, a careful saver, a homemaker who chooses creative over costly, and a mom and wife who knows togetherness and tradition are the keys to my happiness—things no amount of money can buy.

AUTHOR'S NOTE: As a writer and blogger, I work as a spokesperson and freelance writer for many stores and brands, including Kenmore, Walmart, ALDI, Kellogg's, and Goodwill. Despite having these relationships, I will always be honest and truthful about what options work best for my family and what products and stores I truly recommend to save on your family budget. All opinions and thoughts on these products and services are my own and are in no way a reflection of my relationship with any company.

# 1

## The Budget: Make It, Live It, Love It

I have enough money to last me the rest of my life—
unless I buy something . . .

—JACKIE MASON

As a young woman and a mom, I've been offered countless nuggets of advice—good, bad, helpful, and just plain silly. Though much of it hasn't made a lasting impression, a few of the gems have stuck with me: "Be kind to others." "Get your education." "Never put off until tomorrow what you can do today." Those all made sense, and I did my best to remember and to try to follow them.

Unfortunately, there are also some bits of advice I wish I'd listened to right from the get-go, like "Never spend what you haven't got," and that Benjamin Franklin classic, passed on by mothers and teachers everywhere: "A penny saved is a penny earned." They're such simple concepts, and so completely common sense, but alas, not popular with very many twentysomething newlyweds starting out and only seeing bigger and better things ahead.

When a sudden job loss came into our lives, my husband and I had to regroup and start over with a new appreciation for saving and frugal spending. By then, we were not at square one, but rather somewhere quite far behind it, needing to clear out a mounting debt before we could even think about finding some pennies to save.

In the long run, learning the art of budgeting changed my life for the better. After a very rough couple of years, we found our way back to a semblance of financial stability. By then, I'd learned to cut corners, even when it seemed there were no corners left to trim. I'd learned that there are countless ways to save every day, every week, and every month—and that most of them are not that hard to swallow. I learned that even the toughest budget cuts are far easier to accept than the strain and stress of coming up short when it's time to pay the mortgage or the utility bills at the end of the month.

Believe me when I say it: A smart budget shouldn't be the tool you resort to in times of crisis. It should be a permanent, essential piece in the building of your happy home. The keys to getting your budget in order are neither fun nor simple, but once you've got a handle on it, you'll feel like you are in control of your money—rather than feeling like you're chasing and losing it all the time! After struggling, learning, and finally accepting that we choose to live on a budget—not just temporarily, but always—our family is living frugally, and happily, ever after.

Any good budget starts with the first step of taking an unflinching look at your income and spending habits and figuring out how you allot your resources (and how you want to allot them). Once you've got a clear picture of where the money goes, you can start whittling away at your debts, bills, and spending.

# Step 1: Get Up Close and Personal with Your Finances

Family finances are kind of like fingerprints—no two are exactly the same. Some families, like ours, have income that fluctuates from month to month and year to year. Some live on a fixed income. Spending priorities range from things like a big house or a safe car to private school tuition, retirement savings, or trying to put enough food on the table for a houseful of hungry teenagers.

One thing that many families have in common, though, is a tendency to inaccurately estimate pieces of their financial picture. The statistics are all over the place, but one recent study reported that 75 percent of respondents underestimate their monthly spending. Another found that consumers estimate their credit card debt at about half of what it actually is. There is a big disconnect for many of us between what our actual financial picture looks like and how we perceive it. So, the first step in any good budget involves getting intimate—and honest—about what you have, what you owe, and what you are spending.

## KNOW WHAT YOU HAVE

To be fair, I guess we all have days when we might like to deny the basic facts: our weight, for example; our age; or how much we owe on our American Express. For me, the time for taking a hard look at our finances came when it seemed money was flowing through our hands and we didn't have enough to cover the bills. Any time is a good time to make a financial assessment, but if you are using credit cards to bridge the gap from month to month or just to get by, the sooner, the better, because this kind of debt can be like quicksand, pulling you in deeper and deeper over time.

Start by sitting down with everyone in the family who earns or spends money and making a basic assessment of monthly net income (the amount each person brings home from each paycheck per month). One Federal Reserve study found that single people in general had a better idea of how much debt they had, presumably since they are in sole control of their expenses. If a couple shares income and expenses, both parties need to be in agreement about any budget for it to work. Gather your pay stubs, bank statements, and bills. Calculate your total monthly credit card debt and any other outstanding accounts that don't equate to fixed, monthly payments.

## CREATE A FAMILY BUDGET BOOK

To really figure out where your money goes, you need to keep track of every dollar for a month or more. Yes, this is a pain in the neck, but it's the only way to be able to visually see what's happening to your funds. A pocket-sized notebook works perfectly for this job (as long as each money-spending member of your family keeps one). If you have a smartphone, you can keep a running memo, email, or document with your expenditures in it so you can add them up at the end of each day or week. Or you can download a free printable worksheet—or use one of the many free interactive family budget calculators online.

When you put together your spending log, don't forget to include bills you only pay quarterly, twice a year, or annually. These expenses—things like insurance payments, auto registrations, and exterminator contracts, all add up. Other easily left out expenses include gifts, drugstore items, take-out food, and auto mainte-

## GREAT GEEKY IDEAS

### Mint.com

I've always been a pen-and-paper girl, especially when I'm try-ing to sort something out and make sense of it. That said, drawing a pie chart isn't one of my specialties, to say the least. Neither is making sure every single receipt ends up accounted for on my monthly spending chart. Despite clinging to my pen and paper, I also use Mint.com, a free, online financial manager that makes it much easier to keep track of our family's expenses and to set up budgets based on historical spending.

One of the best things about Mint.com is that it can link to any account—including bank accounts and debit or credit cards—and automatically categorizes the easily identifiable ex-penses like groceries, gas, and utilities. A simple click turns your spending into a chart so you can easily visualize where your money goes. In addition, it can turn your historical spend-ing into a monthly budget, and you can fine-tune it from there.

nance. By writing down every little thing, you'll start to get a clear illustration of what is being spent where.

## FIND YOUR SPENDING LEAKS

Creating a livable budget means assessing every aspect of your earning and spending—both fixed expenses and flexible ones. As you're creating your family budget book and writing down ex-penses, keep an eye out for your personal spending weaknesses that need to be identified. Everybody has areas where spending seems to slip "under the radar," and even the smallest of these can really add up. Personally, once I started looking, I found that the vague category of "trips to Target" was costing us a small fortune. Going out for coffee was adding up to a lot, too. Most of all, my grocery spending was out of control. It was (and still is!) all too easy to go out for a gallon of milk and come home with a hundred dollars' worth of unneeded food.

---

## TAKE FIVE

### Five Ways to Teach Your Children to Be Frugal

Raising my children to be frugal is important to me for so many reasons. I want them to understand that resources are limited, that people have to earn the things they want and need, and that they need to grow up to be responsible and self-supporting. I hope they will learn from their dad and me that being frugal is a wise choice, and one they can be proud of. To help your kids learn to be smart about money, try keeping these five lessons in mind:

■ **Teach them to spend.** The easiest way to give kids the impression that money is something vague and always available is have them constantly watch you swipe your credit card. If you want to teach your kids to be frugal and be good stewards of their money, make a point of comparison shopping, then paying with carefully counted-out cash. To really help them understand, take them shopping at a thrift store, garage sale, or other low-cost venue with a couple of dollars of their own and help them make smart selections.

■ **Don't waste.** And explain to your kids why they shouldn't be wasteful, either. We live in a world that's full of disposable stuff, and I think we have a responsibility to teach our children to take care of their belongings and only use what they need. When a toy gets broken, try to fix it instead of automatically replacing it. When your children outgrow their clothes and shoes, let them help clean, fold, and sort them to be handed down or donated.

- **Show them some things are worth the wait.** Delaying gratification may be one of the most important things you can teach your children. When kids have a chance to want and wait (and save) for things that matter to them, they appreciate them more, and they begin to understand a concept that will one day help them into their first car and first mortgage. You can teach your children by showing them how you wait and save for things you want, and also by encouraging them to work toward things they want.

- **Share some details.** You don't have to (and shouldn't) explain all your financial details and woes to your kids, but you should help them gain some perspective on where the family's money goes. Explain why you are buying what you've chosen and make the kids a part of the process. Help them understand that being frugal doesn't mean living without rewards—it just means being smart about how and how much you spend. A pie chart of household expense categories is a great way to offer an easy-to-understand visual for a middle-grade child (or even one much older than that).

- **Be honest.** If your family is struggling with financial issues, talk to your child about the choices you are making to overcome them. Ryan and I chipped away at our credit card debt for years, and we tried to be as open as possible with our children about what we were working for and why. They understood we were cutting corners in other parts of our budget to pay our debt. When we finally settled the last of it, we threw a paying-off-the-credit-card party with the kids. They knew they had been part of our family's sacrifice to dig out from under that debt, and we wanted them to feel a part of the success, too.

Pinpointing your spending pitfalls doesn't necessarily mean giving up things you enjoy or splurge on. Instead, it means recognizing them, considering them in the big picture of your budget, then *choosing* what is and is not worth your extra cash.

## VISUALIZE YOUR BUDGET PIE

If seeing is believing, then there may be no more powerful budgeting tool than a simple pie chart. This visual aid—the one we use to help children understand how the parts of a whole are divided—is just the in-your-face tool I need sometimes when one piece of our family's budget starts taking up too much of the whole. Our pie has changed drastically since we were newlyweds, when it seemed big housing and eating-out budgets were perfectly reasonable, and savings was such a tiny sliver on our chart it might not have been visible to the naked eye.

A look at the average American household's basic budget can help put your own spending in perspective. Consider these typical major monthly expense averages (after taxes) from the U.S. Bureau of Labor Statistics:

- **Housing:** 34 percent. The average family spends the biggest portion of their income on housing and related utilities.

- **Auto, gas, and transportation:** 17 percent. For the lucky few who work close to home, this expense may be as low as 10 percent, but for those with long commutes, it can easily exceed 20 percent.

- **Food:** 13 percent. When you add up both store-bought food and restaurant and take-out meals, the average American family spends an average of 12 to 15 percent of their income on what they eat. This is far less than what our grandparents and great-grandparents spent on food—an average of around 30 percent of their income. There's a big catch here, though, and it's one we need to all remember both as consumers and as compassionate neighbors. The lower a family's income is, the more likely they are spending a higher percentage of income on food. In many low-income families, food is the biggest single expense in the budget, outpacing even housing.

- **Personal insurance and pensions:** 10 percent.

- **Health care:** 6 to 7 percent.

- **Entertainment, education, clothing, services, and miscellaneous:** 18 percent. While some costs in this area, like student loans and child-care expenses, are fixed, this broad category and that of food spending are the ones where most families can pare down costs when the budget gets tight. In our household, I break it down into spending in categories like gifts ($25/month), entertainment ($60/month), "mad money" ($40/month), and clothes ($40/month). I make sure to monitor how much of our "pie" this spending takes up from month to month, in case we need to make adjustments.

## SHAKE UP YOUR SPENDING HABITS

I think budgeting is a lot like dieting. If you go all out on some crazy starvation scheme, you're not likely to stick to it. If you make small changes and learn to live with them, you're more likely to stay focused on and meet your long-term goals. Also, every budgeter (and every dieter) slips up from time to time. The most important thing is knowing that living within your means is important to you and learning what your personal pitfalls are and how to avoid them. For so many of us, the first big step in changing our spending habits is finding a way to be truly conscious of them. I recommend trying one of these spending shake-ups for a month:

**Become a cash-only consumer.** There's no arguing against the convenience of credit cards—a little piece of plastic in your pocket that can cover the cost of anything is much easier to manage than a wad of cash that has to be apportioned, reckoned with, and held in reserve for a greater need. Cash spending is, as one psychological study put it, "transparent," while spending with credit offers just enough of the illusion of there being plenty of resources to go around to get us into trouble.

**Spend a month on the envelope system.** This age-old system is one that is believed to have been popular during the Depression, when banks weren't necessarily considered the safest place to keep one's money anyway. Today, financial guru Dave Ramsey and many others advocate it because it gets down to the nitty-gritty of learning how to spend only what you have.

The envelope system relies on the very basic premise that most people don't spend as much in cash as they do with other forms of payment. Here's how it works: At the beginning of the month (or the week, if you want to start small), allocate the money for your major bills and pay them as you normally would. Then, decide how much money you want to budget for all the other spending in your life—groceries, dining out, apparel, drugstore items, entertainment, gifts, gas, and so on. Now withdraw the amount you've allowed yourself from the bank, and put each budget—in cash—into an envelope labeled for that category of expenses.

Spend only what's in each envelope. If you can shuffle money between envelopes without shortchanging another expense, that's allowed, but withdrawing more money or getting out your credit card makes the system a complete bust! It may actually take more than one month to figure out how to get by on just the cash you give yourself, but this exercise can really help put spending in perspective for any family.

## FAMILY TRADITIONS

### Take a No-Spend Challenge

One of the tools that has best helped me to assess and reconsider my spending habits is occasionally taking what I call a No-Spend Challenge. After trying out an occasional money-free weekend and doing pretty well, my husband and I first tried this experiment a few years ago in February. I chose February because, well, it's the shortest month! Plus, we don't have any birthdays or other big extra expenses that month.

We set aside a modest gas and grocery budget and paid our fixed bills as usual. Other than that, though, we committed to not spending *any money* for the whole month. No incidental spending on a coffee with the girls, no trips to Hobby Lobby, no books, no unnecessary toiletries, no movie tickets, no Happy Meals, no—you get the idea. I know it sounds tough, but we approached it like an adventure—something along the lines of going camping in the backyard.

We enlisted our kids to help come up with fun ways to pass the extra time we'd have, since we would not be spending any of ours shopping. Their ideas included breaking out our board games, making a treat from ingredients in the pantry, watching some of our long-neglected DVDs, cleaning out the laundry room (that one was my idea!), and going to the library.

I'm not going to lie and say it was easy, but at the end of the month we had spent a grand total of just fifty-five dollars in discretionary funds. Along the way, I realized that while I was choosing not to spend, I was able to truly appreciate how plentiful my life already is. Instead of thinking about the things I wished I could buy, I discovered how little I need to be happy.

As consumers, we become conditioned to spend, spend, spend, so that initial week of our challenge proved difficult, but getting over the hump and feeling the success of breaking our spending cycle felt fantastic for both me and my husband.

A no-spend month does come with challenges, but it also comes with the gratification of knowing that you have let your bank account grow and become more aware of where your money is going.

# Step 2: Cut Back on the Big and Small

Choosing where and when to spend your money is a deeply personal decision, and choosing where to scrimp and when to splurge is, too. But no matter what your priorities are, you can find ways to save money and cut your budget, on both the seemingly fixed bills and those that are much more fluid. Consider these tips:

## CHECK AND DOUBLE-CHECK EVERY BILL

Never take anyone else's word for what you owe without carefully checking over every bill yourself. Phone service providers, cable companies, medical billers, and even utility companies routinely make mistakes. A friend of mine received a $630 electric bill for one summer month—more than double an average bill. She asked for a reassessment, and a meter reading revealed she owed less than half of that total. The electric company—like most of the people who bill you—didn't care either way. They simply pushed the numbers, right or wrong, down to the consumer and expected her to pay until they were corrected.

Phone companies are notorious for making changes to user plans and then billing for them—even if you haven't spoken with a representative. Perhaps the most likely area to find a billing error, though, is in medical invoices. Multiple reviews of these bills have found them riddled with errors. Estimates range from 40 percent of bills having errors to 90 percent. Either percentage—or any number in between—represents a billing system that is failing the people it serves.

To make sure billing errors aren't cutting into your budget, review every incoming invoice carefully, and watch for any red flags that suggest something is not quite right. Among these:

**Any change in service.** Sometimes a company starts billing you for a service you did not request; in other cases you may cancel a service but find you're still being billed. For example, cell phone providers sometimes send out a bill that charges per-minute, or per-text, rather than the flat rate you agreed to. These kinds of charges need to be discovered right away, because otherwise you could receive months' worth of inaccurate bills—and the longer the problem goes on, the more difficult it becomes to set it straight when you find it.

**Double billing.** Whether it's an item that gets scanned twice at the checkout counter or a monthly charge or fee that gets added twice on your cable or phone bill, this is one of the most common errors in all areas of billing.

**Ghost billing.** Maybe it's for that extra cable box you haven't got. For the texting plan you didn't order or use. For the phone calls you didn't make from your hotel room. Mystery charges have a way of cropping up on all kinds of bills, and unfortunately, if you don't catch and dispute them quickly, they will get more and more difficult to disprove. It only takes a minute to read a bill from top to bottom, quick-checking each charge. Be sure no ghosts put in appearances on yours.

**Medical bill issues.** There are a couple of things you should look for every time you receive a medical bill to help ensure you're not getting overcharged. First, look for a discounted price. Whether you have medical insurance or are self-pay, you should see an original price, and then either an insurance discount or a self-pay discount. Either way, the discount is usually a hefty percentage of the original charge.

Next, make sure your provider isn't double dipping. Sometimes the same procedure is billed twice on a single invoice, and sometimes it's billed by both a hospital and a doctor—or a visit billed by two different doctors for the same period of time. If you see the same description or code twice for one procedure or visit, follow up with the medical office.

Last, make sure you aren't being billed for anything you didn't buy. The medical codes on your bill can be checked for free on the American Medical Association website (search Google for "AMA code value search" to find a link). Sometimes things like X-rays, ultrasounds, or office procedures can end up on your bill, even if you didn't have them done!

## SAVE ON UTILITIES

Yes, I am a penny-pincher, and proud of it, but no, I'm not one of those folks who will sit in the dark to save the cost of burning a light bulb. When it comes to saving money on utilities, I try hard to be well-informed enough to cut corners in the areas where it makes the biggest difference in our bottom line. Here are a few suggestions for cutting your costs on cable and phone bills, electricity, heating oil, and water bills:

**Rethink your phone needs.** Every family's phone needs are different—from just a house phone for one to cell phones for a pair of adults and a houseful of teenagers. No matter how much phone you need, though, there's a good chance you can reduce your spending in this area.

If everyone in your house has a cell phone, then you might ask yourself why you're still paying for a landline. You could just turn it off, or you can switch to a free (or nearly free) phone service like Skype, Vonage, or OBi, which works using your Internet service. As an added bonus, solicitors will have a difficult-to-impossible time getting your number through these services, so you won't have so many unwanted calls.

When we turned off our house phone, our immediate savings was forty dollars each month—money I'd much rather save or spend on something we really want.

Take a look at your family's recent cell phone bills. If you aren't using them much for talking (like a tween's "for emergencies" phone) consider switching to a prepaid plan instead. If you talk less than two hundred minutes a month, you can probably save money. Also, if you are a texter, compare your usage rate to the unlimited texting price to see if you might save money paying the flat fee.

**Consider cable changes.** A few months ago our family made the radical decision to turn off our cable TV service. For a family of admitted television junkies, this was a bold, maybe even risky move. I was a little worried I'd go through Food Network and HGTV withdrawals! Before you go feeling sorry for me, let me tell you that we didn't actually stop receiving or watching television completely, we just cut loose our cable service—to the tune of about seventy dollars a month in savings.

While going cold turkey on cable television is one way to save a bunch on your monthly expenses, there are an increasing number of options for families who are willing to think a little bit outside the box when it comes to television. The first of these is a digital antenna. This is not your parents' (or grandparents') antenna. Unlike the rabbit ears and similar contraptions of our distant memories, a digital antenna is a streamlined, lightweight gadget that can pick up local channels—including high definition feeds—almost anywhere. For about a forty-dollar one-time cost, one of these antennas is not going to offer channels to rival a big package with your cable provider, but in most places it will pick up the major networks and several other channels. In our house, the antenna pulls in twenty-eight channels—not bad for a family that no longer has a cable bill.

Other options to traditional cable include Internet streaming subscription services like Hulu Plus and Netflix. At a few dollars a month, either (or both) are a great bargain compared to "old school" cable and offer a wealth of movies and TV shows on demand.

**Know what your appliances cost.** Do you know which of your electronics and appliances cost the most to run? In most homes, the biggest energy burners are first the heat/air-conditioning system, and then the hot water heater. A hair dryer uses as much power as a clothes dryer, and sometimes more—but most of us don't run our hair appliances as much as the laundry machines.

An easy way to take a chunk out of your electric bill (or gas, depending on your appliance) is simply to launder everything in cold water. This simple change can save between 50 and 90 percent of the electricity of doing a load of wash. There's no need to have your hot water heater working overtime just for your clothes. Save the hot water for the dirty children and husbands—they'll appreciate it more!

Hanging clothes out to dry will save another good-sized portion of your electric bill. You can still use the dryer to get soft, fluffy clothes—just put your clothes in it for five minutes after they're dry or almost dry rather than running a whole cycle.

**Bathe less.** Just kidding! My family is frugal, but we're still squeaky clean. Rather than cutting back on bathing in general, nudge your family toward more showers and fewer baths. As great as a long, soaking bubble bath may be, the fact is that on average it uses two to three times as much water as a quick shower. An average-sized full tub can require up to fifty gallons of water. A low-flow showerhead uses about two and a half gallons per minute, so a five-minute shower uses twelve and a half gallons, and a ten-minute shower uses twenty-five—still far shy of the hot water it takes for a bath.

Also, if your children are like mine, getting them into the shower takes an act of Congress—but getting them out takes another. Get a kitchen timer from the dollar store and teach your kids to set it for five minutes when they shower—plenty of time to get clean without running up both the electric bill and the water bill, too.

## CALCULATE YOUR PERSONAL "LATTE FACTOR"

David Bach, author of *Debt-Free for Life* and the Finish Rich books, coined the term "Latte Factor" to describe the way small indulgences and expenses add up to a lot of money down the drain in splurges. The concept is really simple, but many of us never stop to account for the little things we spend on. Consider the example of a three-day-a-week Starbucks habit. At $3.80 a latte, you will spend $11.40 a week, $45.60 a month, $547.20 a year, and $5,472 over a ten-year period on take-out coffee.

Salon services like manicures, pedicures, and expensive hair treatments are another potentially draining expense that adds up over the long haul. Ditto for fast-food lunches, lottery tickets, ATM fees, Slurpees—all the little indulgences that might not be included in your budget calculations.

I think everyone needs an occasional splurge and should enjoy it without feeling guilty. The issue that comes up when you consider the latte factor, though, is that many of us aren't counting these as expenses and considering how that money could be put to better use. Sometimes it's easier to recognize this kind of spending in others than it is in ourselves! I read one blog written by a man who decided he would put an extra six dollars toward his car payment every time he saw his wasteful coworker arrive at work with a big ol' six-dollar mocha. After a year and a half, he paid off his car—more than a year early! I'd never considered using someone *else's* latte factor for my own benefit, but this enterprising guy found a way.

We all owe it to ourselves to know what we spend and make conscious choices when we decide to indulge—instead of just blindly racking up big tallies on items that might not be worth it to us.

## BARTER AND SWAP YOUR WAY TO SAVINGS

As a child, I was greatly influenced by my father in the art of bartering your talents for the things you desire. He worked in heating and air-conditioning, and I remember that he would help a local restaurant maintain their heating and air in exchange for dinners for our family. I still remember how delicious the root beers and burgers we ate there tasted, and I bet that they tasted even better to my dad, who didn't have to pay for them.

My family applies the same philosophy of bartering and swapping for the things that we want in our lives. It has served us well over the years and has given us a chance to update our home, clothe our family well, and pursue extracurricular activities that we would not have been able to afford otherwise.

**Consider your talents**. Everyone has talents, and taking stock of what you are good at can give you leverage when bartering your services. Are you a fabulous photographer? Do you have a knack for baking? Do you enjoy gardening and maintaining your lawn? Do you craft? Think about how you might be able to trade talents with someone who has a skill you admire or need.

**Pitch your idea.** I hate confrontation as much as the next person, but ask for what you want and see if the other party is interested in exchanging services. I have been known to knit hats in exchange for my Starbucks fix, exchange advertising services on my site for a clothing budget or music/art classes for my children, and we even negotiated a renovation on our home with my husband's web design services. If you never ask, you won't know how much you could save your family.

**Swap with other families.** Bartering isn't the only way to get something for free. Consider starting a swapping network with your friends. Think of the things in your life that cost your family a lot of money—like babysitting, entertainment expenses, and clothing your children. Try swapping with other families, to everyone's benefit.

## THE BEST MOMADVICE

### Confronting the Green-Eyed Monster

In a book about living a good life on a budget, based on my blog about life on a budget, I'd be dishonest if I didn't admit there have been times since my family started on our path to financial responsibility that I've been a little haunted by the road not taken, by jealousy of friends who splurge on things as small as a glass of fine wine in a restaurant, or as big as a house that could swallow my house whole. We live in a culture where bigger is better and competition is everywhere—both out in the open and tucked into the corners of our lives. No matter how good a judge of character you are, there's always going to be someone in your inner circle who seems to be "keeping score"—of who's taking the big vacation, who's paying private tuition, who's got a new car or a designer handbag on her arm.

For some of these people, jealousy is a way of life. For me, it has become a passing feeling, one that I combat every time by remembering why I love my life, and the frugality of it, more than any indulgence I could ever buy. I want to share some of the ways I keep the green-eyed monster at bay and work on finding inner peace with what I have.

## Think About the Maintenance

When I think about adding possessions to my life, I also think about what will be required of me to care for them. A bigger home, for example, means more cleaning. Seeing as I have some difficulty maintaining and keeping up with the things that we already have, I realize a new house would make things much more difficult for me financially, and the added space would not be as rewarding as what I already possess.

When I feel the urge to shop, out of boredom or out of envy, I try to think of things I already have and how I can take care of them. My house is an endless supply of odd jobs and cleaning or organizing projects. Making a list of these things, I can focus my energy on what I have and need to do, instead of what I think I still need.

When my house is tidy and organized, I feel happy with exactly what I have. A sense of order can be a much more satisfying feeling than buying and trying to find a place for another bag of stuff.

### Create Traditions

Our children may also have trouble with jealousy, and so we try to take the focus off buying things and put it on traditions we can create as a family. Instead of loading them up with toys and gadgets, we come up with ways to spend time with them and show them how important family is.

We create traditions that don't cost a lot—like having a pizza night, making crafts together, having a special activity night with one parent, making holiday traditions, and being together as a family. The things I remember from my own child-hood are the traditions from my family—not the stuff they bought me. These are the kinds of things that I want my children to be focused on.

### Gratitude and Goals

One of the things that most helps me with my jealousy is focus-ing on my gratitude for what I already have and the goals I have for my personal life and my career. I found a pretty journal at our local dollar store and started making a list of all of the things that I love about my life already. When I feel jealousy creeping back in, I work on that list, and quickly realize my life is over-flowing with the kinds of blessings that no amount of money could ever buy, and I'd be wise to count them and be happy!

# Step 3: Shop Smarter to Save Money on Everything

Shopping is the most flexible spending category in any household budget, and reducing in this area can save you hundreds of dollars every month. You can achieve most of that savings with smart planning, stockpiling, and knowing how to make the most of sales, coupons, and rebates. What you *don't* have to do to save a small fortune in shopping expenditures is drive to every store, every week, with every coupon you can find. As a busy mom, I try not to take, or make, suggestions that burn up more time than they're worth. Chasing down every bargain means losing time with your family. Shifting your focus to planning ahead and shopping smart will save you both dollars and hours in the long run.

## NEVER UNDERESTIMATE THE POWER OF A GOOD LIST

No matter where or how you shop, the key to keeping spending under control lies in the same simple step: Decide what you are going to buy and how much you are going to spend, and stick to it. Everything from a trip to the dollar store to a day at the mall can bust your budget if you don't have a clear plan. This is just as important when you are going to a thrift shop or a warehouse club as it is at the grocery store. I often have to remind myself that just because something is a great deal doesn't mean it should come home with me. If this is hard for you, put a small "surprise me" on your list—but be sure to give it a price limit and stick to it.

## MAKE FEWER TRIPS TO THE STORE, EVEN IF YOU SPEND MORE PER TRIP

One study found that shoppers who make a quick trip to the store usually spend at least 50 percent more than what they planned. Even if you're not the type to spend that much over your trip budget, the extras that fall or jump into your basket can really add up with every extra shopping outing. For example, if you go to the store three times a week and spend an extra $15 each time, that adds up to $2,340 a year. If you go to the store just once a week and go over budget by the same $15 each time, you'll spend $780 a year on the extras. Savings by just going to the store less often: $1,560 in one year.

The same concept applies whether you are going to the grocery store, a big-box store, the craft shop, or the mall—simply go less often, and you'll spend less overall.

## TAKE ADVANTAGE OF ONLINE FREEBIES

Ebates.com, Swagbucks.com, and other websites offer ways to get discounts, money back, and bonuses for shopping and surfing the Internet. As with any online offer, you always need to be careful to make sure you know who you're dealing with and whether a site is reputable. Both Ebates and Swagbucks work for me and have strong subscriberships and security protections. Ebates is a shopping site that links to hundreds of different online retailers and offers a percentage of your purchases as cash back from each site. Stores include everything from Walmart (1 percent cash back) and Kohl's (6 percent) to Petco (5 percent) and Target (3 percent). In addition to sending you a check every three months with the cash back you earn, the site also helps you find coupons and deals with its member stores.

Swagbucks is a search site that gives you points for using their services instead of other sites like Google. Over time, your points accumulate and you can use them for gift cards or even Paypal deposits into your account. Since I spend quite a lot of time doing research and reading on the Internet, I can rack up as many as four hundred Swagbucks each month. I mostly save my Swagbucks to use toward birthday presents for my kids. If you spend a lot of time on the Internet, you can definitely earn some free stuff here.

## SAVE WITH A BIG-BOX MEMBERSHIP

Having a wholesale club membership at places like Costco, BJ's, or Sam's Club can save you a bundle, but only if you shop smart. Unfortunately, not every bulk price is a bargain—not even close. In order to figure out which items are really deals and which cost as much or more than your neighborhood grocer or department store, you have to be able to compare "apples to apples," to figure out the unit price. For example, many over-the-counter medications are a great deal at wholesale clubs—but the only way to be sure you're getting a bargain is to calculate the per-pill/dose price.

Consider this comparison: a popular allergy medication sells for about $14 at my local drugstore for a forty-five-dose bottle. The generic version of this same medication is available for about $10. At BJ's, the same medication, same dose, in a generic bottle is sold with a store coupon for $11 for three hundred doses. When you break down the prices, that's $0.31 per dose in the first bottle, $0.24 per dose in the second, and less than $0.04 per dose in the last. The savings on this particular drug are huge. Many medications, vitamins, and supplements are offered at big savings from warehouse stores—just make sure you do the per-dose math so you know you're getting the best price.

Always keep a calculator handy when you hit the warehouse store so you can quickly figure out which "deals" are legit and which would be a waste.

Each warehouse chain has its own unique perks—Costco is well known for its great selection, BJ's accepts all manufacturer's coupons, and Sam's Club has a great time-saving program called Click 'n' Pull. Basically, you place your order online before 5 p.m., and the store emails you when it is ready to pick up the next day. I find there are two big advantages to using this system: First, I comparison shop much more efficiently online than I do in the store, where there are so many things to take in and distract me (and tempt me to impulse buy!); second, I can save a lot of shopping time by not having to walk through the store looking for each item one at a time.

Some frequently found best deals at stores like Sam's Club, Costco, and BJ's, include the following:

**Electronics.** It's easy to compare prices on things like computers, cameras, phones, and the like, and many warehouse prices beat even online competitors by a few dollars. One more thing to consider when you choose a vendor is that warehouse stores often have more generous and longer-term returns policies than more traditional electronics retailers.

**Meat.** The per-pound price of meat at wholesale clubs is often 20 percent or so less than the regular grocery store price. In addition, I've found the quality of the meat at my wholesalers' counter is usually better than at the regular market. Most warehouse packages contain more meat than my family would ever eat for a single meal, but by dividing the big packs and freezing family-of-four-size portions, I get the most for my meat budget. Be sure to ask the butcher if he will divide these packages up for you, saving you the time and money required to package the meat yourself.

**Rice, dried beans, grains, and pantry staples like flour and sugar.** All these cooking supplies with long shelf lives can be bought at a solid discount—in bulk—at any wholesale club. The catch, as with any product you buy, is to be sure you will use all you purchase before its expiration date.

**Bread, cheese, milk, butter.** If you use any of these staples in quantity, you'll be hard-pressed to beat warehouse club prices on their store-brand varieties. For example: at this writing a pound of butter at my local grocery store costs $3.49 ($3.49 per pound). A package containing four pounds of store-brand butter sells at the local warehouse store for $8.39 ($2.09 per pound).

**Paper products.** Even at a warehouse store, the price of brand-name paper products is extreme. In fact, sometimes it is higher than the per-unit price in a department store or at your local market. The store-brand products, though, are often the best deal around for things like paper towels, toilet paper, and paper plates.

## SAVE ON CLOTHES AND SHOES

Shopping off-season is one of the most frugal ways to outfit your family for half price or less. Almost every retail store deeply discounts clothing and shoes at the end of each season, and if you are dressing growing kids, thinking a few months ahead can save you a fortune. As for us adults, I try to add a few things to my wardrobe once or twice a year, but since my size isn't changing (fingers crossed) I'm happy to wait until I find the just-right item at the just-right price.

In addition to saving on kids' clothes at the clearance racks, don't forget to check thrift stores and yard sales. Just like your children outgrow most of their clothes before they wear them out, so do everyone else's kids. Secondhand clothes for kids are often in nearly new condition.

One of my favorite ways to refresh a kid's wardrobe is with an organized exchange with my best friend. Each of us keeps a plastic tub for each of our children's outgrown clothes. If an item is in good condition, we wash it, fold it, and stash it away for the next exchange. On exchange day, we trade bins labeled with each child's sex and size, and "shop" for clothes from each other's saved items. This simple, frugal system keeps us both in right-sized, stylish clothes for our children—plus we get to spend an evening catching up and having a glass of wine while we do our shopping. This arrangement can be used with great success by a group of friends who get together for book club or to play Bunco—more moms participating means more clothes, more sizes, and more contributors going home happy.

If a clothing exchange works out among you and your friends, consider other types of exchanges: books, magazines, recipes, and coupons are all great candidates for a swap-night with friends.

## THINK THRIFTY

Thrift-store shopping can be an amazingly inexpensive way to get everything from shoes to toys to furniture and décor items. Shopping for secondhand items can be intimidating for beginners, but there are great deals to be had on good-quality stuff if you know how to go about it.

If you've never been thrifting before, start by getting familiar with your area stores. Take an afternoon and visit the secondhand shops nearby to see what kinds of things they have. In our area, one high-rent neighborhood has a great thrift shop that always has new donations coming in. Some shops price their used merchandise ridiculously high, while others fail to price some things at all. A trip around town to see the different choices will help determine which shops might have treasures waiting for you to find.

Once you've found a store that seems to have nice goods for sale, inquire about coupons and discounts. Stores that make money for charities may offer a coupon in return for a small donation. Others may offer a membership for a small fee—maybe five dollars—in return for a coupon each month. Many shops have discount days, and others have policies for deeply discounting items that have been for sale for more than a couple of weeks. It pays to know your local store's policies.

Just like any other shopping, a list is your friend when you're thrifting. When I first discovered one great little thrift shop, I was so excited about everything I could get so cheaply, I was buying everything I liked and cluttering up my house—never a good idea. Writing down what you need—or creating an inspiration board on paper or on a site like Pinterest—will help you stay focused on what you hope to find.

And there are plenty of treasures out there—small appliances like bread machines and rice cookers, brand-name clothes and shoes, books and games, and home décor items. I especially love thrift shopping for finding great little wardrobe items that would cost a fortune in retail stores—things like fitted jackets and designer jeans. To be honest, some of my favorite pieces in my wardrobe came to me as thrift-store finds.

To get the best selection, hit up thrift shops first thing in the morning. Be nice to the staff and they may tell you which days they put out new donations. No matter what you're buying, take the time to go over the details—checking especially for good seams, matching buttons, and working zippers. Give everything a good scrub before use, and you'll be on your way to becoming an expert at uncovering thrift-store finds.

# Step 4: Pay Down and Save Up

Thinking about your budget in terms of more than just matching up income and bills is a unique challenge when you're on a tight budget. In order to reach any level of financial security for your family, though, you've got to address both debts and savings. For a long time our household had to focus first on paying off debts. If you have credit card balances and are paying interest, you need to deal with those first. The way our family approached it is what some financial gurus call the "snowball method." We paid the minimum balances on our cards except the one with the lowest balance—which we paid with every dime we could scrape together. Once that one was paid off, we continued to pay the same amount, but with the extra cash going to the next balance. In time, we were able to roll our remaining balances to one card, and then to finally exhale once that was paid off. When we were free of credit card debt, we turned our attention to paying our own savings, depositing what had previously been our credit card payment into our own savings account each month.

## CRUNCH YOUR CREDIT

If you've ever visited my blog or read one of my columns, you may already know how I feel about credit cards. I dislike them and they scare me. Our family has already been in serious credit card debt in this lifetime, and after going through the grueling process of digging ourselves out (to the tune of thirteen thousand–plus dollars), we won't let ourselves get into that particular mess again.

Even though I know people who benefit from reward credit cards, I also know those who practice what the credit industry calls "purchase acceleration"—spending more than they would otherwise to gain more rewards on the card. Since reward cards usually have a higher interest rate than non-reward cards (an average of two percentage points), it's ridiculously easy to wipe out any rewards you might earn in extra spending and interest charges. Besides, in many cases you can get the same kind of cash-back rewards with a well-chosen debit card.

Of course, credit cards work just fine for people who pay them off every single month. In addition, there are times when making an exception to a no-credit policy makes sense, even to an avoider like me. First of all, if you have multiple credit cards and are juggling a number of bills and interest rates, it makes sense to consolidate. Shop rates at every lending institution available to you—banks, credit unions, and reputable online lenders. Don't be afraid to get on the phone and ask if you might qualify for a better rate than what is advertised, especially if you have good credit. When we were up to our ears in credit card debt, I was able to find one card that would consolidate most of our debt at one low rate—and that's the one we paid every single month until we were flush again.

Another pretty good deal in the credit card world is the same-as-cash offers available at some stores on big purchases like furniture, appliances, electronics, and home improvement purchases. If you are disciplined enough to pay these accounts off before the deadline—because the interest rates are always sky-high if you don't—then you can parcel out your payments over multiple months (or even years) without any penalty.

## START SAVING

It can be so very difficult to find money to save when you're already living frugally—especially if you're paying off debts. Still, every family needs to have money put away in case of job loss, a family crisis, or a true emergency expense. Our family learned this the hard way, and now we are diligent about saving, no matter what. For some people, using a simple financial gimmick to keep money separate and heading to savings is enough to get the ball rolling. Try one of these tricks to help start your own nest egg:

**Keep the change.** A very simple way to start small savings is to make a habit of paying for everything with bills and accumulating your change as savings. Once a month, roll your change and deposit it into a separate account. Whenever you can afford to drop dollars into your special savings account, add them to the deposit.

**Raise your savings.** If you are a salaried or hourly worker, each time you receive a raise is cause for celebration. Why not celebrate by starting to squirrel away some money in savings? If you receive a 3 percent annual cost-of-living raise, have your bank funnel it into a separate savings account for you. This is money you won't miss if it never gets to your wallet, and it can quickly accumulate to help pay for whatever your financial priority is.

**Keep your rainy-day fund separate.** No matter what you're saving for, setting up a separate account at your bank will help you accomplish it. Ryan and I have been putting twenty-five dollars a month into an anniversary trip account for several years now. We haven't even planned our trip, but the idea of that account slowly growing for our goal makes me feel happy and secure.

## GETTING THROUGH THE TOUGHEST TIMES

I think we all understand that there is a fundamental difference between living on a budget and living paycheck to paycheck—or worse yet, trying to get by without a steady income. In recent years, unemployment has soared in the United States, and more people have been out of work than any time I can remember in my life. The situation affects all kinds of people—educated professionals, people who work hourly blue-collar jobs, and those who work part time or freelance from all walks of life. Our own part of the country in Indiana has been particularly hard hit, and so we know many people, besides ourselves, who have had to deal directly with job loss.

There's no magic system for getting by on less money than you need, but there are a few steps you can take to help keep bill collectors from closing in and banging down your door while you work through it. Consider these suggestions:

**First, call every creditor.** Explain that you have suffered a job loss and ask if there is any way they can defer or forgive your bill for a short time while you get on your feet. A surprising number of creditors can be very helpful if you get in touch with them before you fall behind on your payments. I have a friend who called the cable company to turn off her Internet, phone, and cable service—only to be told that the company would continue it, at no charge, for the first three months of job loss. Mortgage companies have been dealing with a slew of delinquent homeowners in recent years, and most of them are more than willing to work with borrowers who want to stay in their homes and are experiencing temporary loss of income. As you work through the list, you can then organize your priorities: starting with food for your family, your home, and the resources you need to effectively search for a new job.

**Consider your health insurance.** I can honestly say that worrying about health insurance was one of the biggest stressors that came out of our family's period of unemployment. COBRA payments are so astronomically expensive that very few, if any, cash-strapped families can afford them. First, call your state insurance department and ask if they can give you any guidance on finding reasonably priced insurance. Be sure to specifically ask if they have any coverage available for you or for your children while you are unemployed. Many states offer health insurance for children at very low subsidized rates. This may be available for you to sign up for immediately.

**Next, call your doctor.** If you have an established relationship with a practice, they may be willing to do a great deal to help you and may also have direct-pay rates that are deeply discounted. Ask if they have samples or coupons available for the prescriptions you take—these often go unused, believe it or not. If they are not able to treat your family, ask if they can refer you to a doctor who will. Remember that low-cost cash clinic chains like Solantic treat most routine and minor health issues for reasonable rates.

**Find financial planning assistance.** No one needs financial assistance more than someone who is struggling to make ends meet. Contact your local library and see if there are any charitable organizations or financial planners that donate their services to low-income families. See if you can get guidance on how to make the most of the budget you are in and what you can do to protect yourself from falling further into debt.

**Know your rights.** Even if someone is trying to collect a legitimate debt from you, it is important to understand your rights and what is and is not allowed when it comes to debt collection. The Fair Debt Collection Practices Act outlines your rights and what debt collectors can and cannot do in order to collect an overdue balance. If you feel you are being harassed or treated unfairly, you can file a complaint with the Federal Trade Commission (1-877-382-4357).

## THE BEST MOMADVICE

### Helping an Unemployed Friend

Our family endured almost a year of unemployment and a mountain of credit card debt that came with it. I often look back on that time in our lives and wonder how we ever got through it with our marriage, our faith, and our optimism intact. Based on our experience, these are my suggestions for reaching out to help an unemployed friend.

**Lend an Ear**

The most important thing you can do for someone who is having a hard time financially is to just let them talk. Let them share their anger or grief or frustration with the struggles they are enduring, and celebrate with them when those times turn around. Let them talk about what they feel like talking about, and try not to push them to tell more than they feel comfortable with.

**Offer to Babysit**

The number one cause of divorce is money problems. When a spouse is unemployed, particularly the male in the family, it is such a difficult time in a marriage because so much of one's pride and self-esteem comes from being able to contribute financially to the family.

The best thing you can do to keep that marriage growing strong is offer to support them by babysitting. Give the family the time they need to have a date night or the chance to quietly do some job searching. If you have the finances to offer a gift card for a night out, that is a wonderful and thoughtful touch. Think of fun, budget-friendly things they could do like going bowling, or a gift card to Barnes & Noble for books or coffee, or a gift certificate to the movie theater.

### Meals on Wheels

One of my favorite things to do for people during hard times is just drop off a dinner or bring a meal when I come over to spend time with them. Try to make a big batch of food that could get them through one or two nights when money is tight. If you lack the cooking gene, head over to the supermarket and pick up a take-and-bake pizza, popcorn, and some break-and-bake cookies. These are likely fun foods that have been removed from the grocery budget and will be just as much appreciated as a home-cooked meal.

### Be an Anonymous Giver

Pride gets in the way of sometimes getting the help that someone might need. No one wants to say, "I don't have money for groceries this month." I have some very proud people in my life who would never tell me when they were struggling. I have learned that anonymous gifts, like a gift card in the mail, are sometimes the best kinds of gifts to give in these situations.

# 2

# The Frugal, Generous Kitchen

have a confession to make. There was a time, not that long ago, when I thought beef stew was something invented by a guy named Dinty Moore—and not only did he invent it, he must have had a patent, because, honestly, how often had I ever encountered beef stew outside of a can?

Let's just say I've come a long way since then. At twenty-two, I could barely make boxed macaroni and cheese. These days, I plan tasty, healthy meals and snacks for my family, and I make pretty much everything from scratch. My transformation didn't happen because I'd always wanted to be like Martha Stewart. It started because our household suddenly became kind of poor—and we cut the take-out and quick-prepare meals I'd always relied on from our budget. Food is one area where I quickly discovered there's a lot of fat, so to speak, to trim. Deep deductions in grocery spending were a huge help in bringing our family finances down in a hurry.

How much money can a person save by shopping smart and learning to whip up homemade foods instead of pre-prepared fare? Consider this: The government estimates a moderate food budget for a family of four at about $770 a month. I spend less than half of that. Even with food prices rocketing up over the past couple of years, our family continues to eat very well on a grocery budget of between $300 and $350 per month.

The surprising thing, to me, is that I'm pretty sure my family eats as well or better now than when we had a bigger food budget. Planning ahead and cooking homemade meals helps me ensure that the food I put on the table is not just appetizing but also nutritious. As my kids get older, I'm very glad most of the foods they eat come from my own kitchen—not a big factory where chemical additives and preservatives are basic ingredients. Taking a couple of cooking classes has also helped me see that with a little creativity and research, I really can make anything in my kitchen at home. I may have started out as a grown woman who thought beef stew only came in a can, but today I can make not only soups and stews but also my own breads and baked goods, sauces and spice mixes, and some pretty darned delicious knock-offs of my family's favorite "restaurant" foods—everything from fancy coffees and ice cream to homemade gyros and penne with vodka cream sauce. I guess I'd rate myself as a seven as a cook now—which isn't too shabby considering I started out hovering near a one! Cooking has become more than a necessity for me and more than a way to save on the budget. It's a hobby I continue to get better at and that, most days, I enjoy.

Perhaps most important of all, over the past several years cooking has become an important center of our family life. It is part of what makes our family special, and cooking and having meals together is one of the ways we enjoy time with one another. The routines of planning meals, preparing them, and eating them together help shape our home life. My kids don't just get healthy meals; they are also learning how to make frugal choices, how to help plan a menu calendar, how to sort and measure ingredients, and how we cook for one another and the important people in our lives with love and care. I hope these are life lessons they will carry with them as they get older and one day have homes and families of their own.

For me, the keys to a well-run, frugal, and loving kitchen are simple: First, plan wisely with a menu calendar and a well-stocked pantry. Second, save your hard-earned money by learning to make almost anything yourself. Third, cook efficiently by using valuable tools, food-prep techniques, and time-saving shortcuts.

## Smart Grocery Shopping

Food spending is one of the most flexible areas in any family's budget, but many of us don't pay close attention to where our grocery dollars are going. So much of food shopping tends to be done on impulse, with quick trips to the market for one item or another resulting in hundreds of dollars in extra spending. Getting the most for your food allowance will go a long way toward keeping overall spending under control. I am amazed sometimes at the checkout counter at how little some people are getting for their money! Here are just a few ways to start cutting back on your food bill:

Never leave home without . . .

**A budget.** When my children were smaller, my grocery budget was firmly set at $50 a week. As they get older and eat more, though, I've started spending more on food. These days, our family spends about $80 per week. That allotment is plenty for me to buy the things we need. Many of my girlfriends readily admit to spending $200, $250, $300, or even more on food each week. That would be fine if they were choosing to do so and happy with it—but mostly they are frustrated and puzzled at where all that money goes. Set an exact dollar amount—per trip, per week, or per month, depending on what's easiest for you—and know you are going to stick to it.

**Cash.** I only take cash to the supermarket, and that simple choice helps keep me on my budget. When you carry a credit card, there just seems to be a bottomless fund, and if you go a teensy bit over . . . well, so what? When dealing in cash, you have to stay within your budget constraints, period. This can help you look at your grocery cart in a whole new light. Suddenly those Twinkies or premade sushi or chips don't seem really necessary—instead, it appears they are taking up important funds that are already earmarked for the groceries you really need.

**Calculator.** If you're going to spend only cash, it's well worth your trouble to bring a calculator to keep a tally of your purchases. Sadly, I've taken my turn being that lady at the checkout station who is setting aside a few things to put back—definitely not the way I like to learn my budget lessons!

## CHOOSE YOUR DEAL(S)

My personal purchasing policy is something along the lines of: If it's not a good bargain, I can wait. Bargains come in lots of different forms, though, and a savvy shopper knows one when she sees one. I'm not a fan of driving to every market for every sale item—this is far too time-consuming and can easily lead to extra purchases I don't need at all. To be honest, I hate to grocery shop, so I only set out once every two or three weeks to do the job. I'm willing to make a couple of stops to get the most for my money, but you won't find me shop-hopping every time a sale flyer comes out.

To get the most of your grocery budget, start by following these simple savings guidelines:

**Visit no-frills markets.** Choosing a grocery store that doesn't offer day care, a fine cheese counter, wine tastings, and the like will save you a fortune in little price hikes on everything from chicken breasts and macaroni to ice cream and canned corn. Shopping at a basic market like ALDI or Save-A-Lot will help you get the best deals in grocery shopping—all for nothing more than showing up. The prices at stores like these often beat even the generics at other markets.

**Price match.** Many stores price match, but few do it more widely and graciously than Walmart, which even matches any generic store brand when selling their Great Value products. You can get some great deals by picking the loss leaders in a number of ads and shopping at just one store that's willing to price match.

**Buy generics.** Not all generic foods are as good as the name brand, but many of them come very close. The cost difference in some items, like brand-name versus generic breakfast cereal, is substantial—often 40 percent or more. When I first started shopping generics, I'd buy one brand for us to try, and if we didn't care for it, I'd try one from another store. When the product is something I know we'll finish sooner or later no matter what, sometimes we have a home taste test to compare a couple of different varieties—a fun way for everyone to try multiple brands and choose a favorite.

Other especially good generic deals include condiments (25 to 50 percent savings), baking staples like flour and sugar (which are federally regulated during production and all almost the same quality), soda, bread, pasta, ice cream, and packaged snacks.

**Study store circulars.** Weekly fliers are my number one source for nabbing grocery savings. Since I faithfully plan my meals around one big shopping trip, what's on sale often determines what my family will be dining on in the coming weeks. Great BOGO (buy one, get one) deals, discounts on meats, seasonal produce specials—these are the staples of my shopping list.

**Clip coupons.** Coupons and I have a mixed relationship. Since I mostly buy generic products, I can usually beat even the coupon price (or even the double coupon price) on a name brand. However, the success of couponing shows and books has me taking a second look and doing the math again. The biggest pitfall of couponing is spending money on things you wouldn't buy anyway—just because they're a great deal. Rather than clip every coupon I find, I rely first on my grocery store flyers—and second on coupons—to get the best deal. If an item is on sale in the flyer, look to match it with a coupon from the same week's circulars. Choose a market that takes double coupons, and you'll be in the same league with the *Extreme Couponing* queens.

**Shop a warehouse club.** Shopping at Sam's Club, BJ's, or Costco can be overwhelming at first. All those huge packages of everything under the sun—not to mention the displays of everything from furniture and toys to rugs and tires. Nevertheless, there are many groceries you can find at better prices in a big-box club than almost anywhere else.

For example, I buy all my baking supplies at a warehouse club store. Flour, sugar, and yeast all cost significantly less there than I can find them in the grocery store. I bake a lot, and I use my bread maker all the time, so my savings in flour and yeast alone is enough to pay for my membership to the club for a whole year. On a recent day, a five-pound bag of flour at the grocery store was selling for $3.85 ($0.77 a pound). A twenty-five-pound bag at my local big-box store was $7.89 ($0.32 a pound). The savings on yeast is even more dramatic: a four-ounce jar at the grocery store costs around $4. A *two-pound* container of the same brand and product at the big-box store costs less than $5! Grocery store price: $1 per ounce. Warehouse club price: about $0.03 per ounce. That kind of savings is worth considering a membership.

## SAVE ON THESE FOODS

I'm always looking for new tips on spending less for the same good groceries. Use these tips to get specific foods at great prices:

**Meat.** Buying your meat in bulk packages from the butcher, a warehouse store, or your grocery store can save you dollars off every pound. I purchase as much as ten pounds of my family's go-to staples when I find a good deal, and then divide the package into one-pound portions for the freezer. A pound is

---

## GREAT GEEKY IDEAS

### Going Postal

I bought a postal scale on eBay that has saved me a lot of time and hassle at the post office. It's also turned out to be surprisingly handy in the kitchen, where I use it to weigh out equal portions of bulk meats for the freezer, as well as weighing ingredients when I cook in bulk.

---

the portion my family typically uses in a meal, but even if I'm making more, the small packages thaw out quickly. (Again, don't forget to ask the butcher if he will subdivide the meat into smaller parcels for you—many times they are happy to provide this service and save you some time.)

**Sandwich meat.** Don't waste your precious grocery money on lunch meat. I purchase a whole turkey once every two weeks and roast one of these for our lunch meat. All I do is put the turkey in a roasting pan, sprinkle a little seasoning on it (salt, pepper, and poultry seasoning), dump a can of chicken broth in the bottom of the roasting pan, and cook till done. We eat half of the meat one week, and the other half goes into the freezer for the following week. Just double bag the meat along with half of a can of chicken broth (to keep it moist) and pop it in the freezer. Once you have a turkey sandwich like this, all of that processed lunch meat won't taste as good and you will never go back. Plus, you'll save between three and seven dollars per pound, depending on your turkey and deli prices. Trust me—I've got all my girlfriends roasting turkeys now!

**Choose eggs.** A dozen eggs usually cost less than two dollars. At times, you can find them on sale or in discount grocers for one dollar or even less. I try to keep two dozen on hand, because this economical staple is a frugal food shopper's best friend. Whether you're trying to stretch your groceries for another day or two, trying to get a meal on the table in ten minutes or less, or just feeding picky kids who don't want anything to do with meat and potatoes, eggs cooked any way you like 'em are the go-to, budget-friendly, "fast" food every mom should never be without.

**Fish for bargains.** Fresh fish, healthy and delicious as it may be, can be a big drain on any grocery budget. Unless you've got a good fisherman in the family, you may find yourself scouring the fish counter for deals that are rarely there. Even though frozen fish may not have all the flavor of a fresh catch, it is a very economical and tasty option for families on a budget. Not only is the price per pound less than the price at the fish counter, but bags of frozen filets sometimes go on sale—even buy one, get one free. Frozen tilapia has become a staple for our family—I can prepare it lots of different ways, and us grown-ups and our kids all enjoy it.

**Buy whole fruits and vegetables.** The convenience of things like precut celery, apple slice packs from the produce section, and baby carrots may all be tempting, but really, how long does it take to cut up a carrot, an apple, or a celery stalk? Ditto for peeled or precooked potatoes. If you compare prices pound per pound, you'll find you are often paying double—and sometimes much more—for a machine to prep these items for you. The savings isn't much per trip to the grocery store, but over time, it really adds up.

**Grow your own.** Not everyone has a green thumb, but growing a few of your own foods will not only take a chunk out of your grocery budget but also help teach your children about where food comes from and how things grow—science plus savings: hooray! I have a small patio garden at my house where I grow my own tomatoes, parsley, basil, rosemary—all easy plants to cultivate. Those fresh herbs can come in on a windowsill in the winter, and they would cost a small fortune to purchase year-round at the market. I try to avoid recipes that call for expensive herbs and spices, but if parsley, basil, or rosemary is featured, I'm happy to add them to my new-dishes-to-try list.

**Save on bakery items.** Even though I love to make my own bread in my bread machine, there is a certain convenience in having a couple of loaves on hand for the unexpected dinner guest or "emergency" sandwich. Instead of reaching for the pricey bread in the bakery aisle, ask your grocer where the rack of day-old items is located. I often find nice loaves of crusty bread and rolls for our family's dinner. This can also be a great place to check if you are the "room mom" in charge of snacks for your child's class. The term "day-old" is often misconstrued as suggesting the food is old or spoiled. This is rarely true. "Day old" usually means the item has a "sell by" date of the day you are buying—and since store-baked goods are made fresh every day anyway, this does not mean the item is stale. It means that tomorrow the store won't be able to sell it at all, and they'd rather take a small loss than a complete one. Some day-old bargains are simply the last items left from a larger display or special. The selection of cakes, cookies, and cupcakes in this section is often wonderful—and the discounts can be half off or more.

**Save on milk.** Although powdered milk is not my favorite thing to drink, it can stretch your grocery budget. Be sure to calculate the price per gallon to compare, but if there is savings in preparing the powdered milk, consider using this for your baking needs. I love to have a gallon of powdered milk on hand to be mixed into recipes like homemade donuts or muffins, as well as added to our favorite waffle and pancake batters. Knowing that powdered milk is in your pantry can also be helpful for those lean cupboard days when a trip to the grocery store is just not on the horizon.

**Make your own baby food.** Although my days of buying baby food are over, one of the things that I did when my children were small was to make my own baby food at home. I would devote one day to making a month's supply, and it saved us loads of money at the grocery store. The process is simple: Visit your local wholesale club for fresh produce, then steam your fruits and vegetables and puree. Assemble in ice trays for individual portions. Once frozen, I stored these in freezer bags for easy grabbing for our little ones. It cost us pennies compared to store-bought baby foods. Most of these foods can be stored up to six months in the freezer. If your children are anything like mine, though, they won't last that long.

**Ditch the disposables.** Did you ever think about how much of your market budget you are actually just throwing away? Disposable napkins, paper plates, wet wipes, and paper towels can drain thirty dollars or more each month on your grocery budget and you have nothing to show for it. We decided to make the switch to cloth napkins, dishrags, and microfiber cloths for our counters, washcloths for little ones' faces, and reusable plates for eating on each day. The cost savings has helped us to stay on better track with our budget, and we also feel good about being environmentally responsible. Try replacing just one of these budget drains and you will see that it is worth your effort.

# Planning Ahead for Breakfast, Lunch, and Dinner

"What's for dinner?" may be the most-asked question in America. Many of us hear it every day. One of the keys to running a frugal kitchen is always having a ready answer.

When we were first married, my husband and I generally started meal planning around the time we got hungry. I never learned to cook when I was growing up, and I wasn't interested as a newlywed. Our grocery shopping method was part "what looks good?" and part "what looks easy?"

The problem with "what looks" meal planning is that you're always running to the store at the last minute, you don't have time to prep food in advance, and you rarely save money on anything. It costs way too much cash and time.

These days, I plan a whole month of meals at a time, then shop twice a month to get everything I need. I can't tell you how much I prefer just going grocery shopping a couple of times a month to going nearly every other day. It may seem daunting to organize that many meals at once, but it's really not that difficult, and once you have a system in place, you can do it in just a few minutes. Here's how to start:

## WRITE IT DOWN

A five-by-eight day planner or pocket calendar is a perfect tool to keep menus straight. Start by filling in just one week's meals on the calendar. A great money-saving way to plan ahead is using the week's grocery circular to choose meals that work around what's on sale. This doesn't have to be time-consuming or complicated—just choose a few key ingredients that are already on sale (like a roast, or a whole chicken, or potatoes) and work around those. Choose five main dishes, and plan for two days of leftovers. Once you've listed your main courses, pick five or six side dishes and vegetables to complement them. Now make your grocery list for all the dishes you chose. It'll be a big list, but saving extra trips to the grocery store—and the money you'd spend on those trips—is worth it. Over time, work up to two weeks of menus.

I make my lists for two weeks at a time, so when I plan my menu, I'm often thinking about timing. If I buy a fresh chicken or fresh fish or a roast, you can bet we'll be having that in week one! In the second week, I focus more on foods from our freezer

### GREAT GEEKY IDEAS

#### Google Docs

I love meal planning with Google documents. This online tool allows any user to create a spreadsheet of meals with links to each of the recipes. I'm up to sixteen weeks of recipes and counting! I can shuffle them around just by dragging and clicking, and I can share recipes via email or my blog just as easily. You can view my calendar at MomAdvice.com—just click on any dish to view the recipe.

and the pantry. Over time, there's a rhythm that develops to meal planning, rotating favorite ingredients, fresh and frozen items, even the use of appliances to create a balance of routine and variety in the family menu.

## GIVE YOURSELF SOME WIGGLE ROOM

Even though I am a planner to my very soul, I'm also juggling two busy kids' schedules, plus my husband's and my own. In a perfect world, when you put "Parmesan Sage-Crusted Pork Chops and Roasted Green Beans" on the calendar for June 20, your family would sit down to that precise meal on June 20, no matter what. For better or worse, "no matter what" is no longer a part of my vocabulary. A busy household has to have some flexibility. So instead of creating a completely fixed menu, I leave a little room for the occasional "moveable feast," moving meals between days and not stressing about it.

One more helpful tool for keeping things flexible is to schedule your main dish for each day of a week, but give yourself a list of side dishes and snacks to work with for that period of time that can be paired with any main dish. I do this for two-week spans on my calendar, and even though I usually just stick to the schedule, it's nice to know any last-minute switches won't mess up the menu for the remainder of the month.

## LOVE YOUR LEFTOVERS

Creative uses for leftovers can give your family a number of meals for little more than the trouble it takes to make one. For example, if you roast a chicken on a Sunday, plan to serve Chicken Broccoli Lo Mein (with leftover chicken, of course) one day that week, and homemade chicken and noodle soup another day. I try to plan my own cooking schedule so I front-load a more labor-intensive meal on the weekend, then give myself the easy-prep meals during the busy week.

A word of advice about recipe selection: Just because you are on a budget doesn't mean you have to limit yourself to basic recipes! It just means you have to focus on recipes with reasonably priced ingredients. When I first started cooking, I was a complete novice, and my exposure to good food was limited, at best. I was trying so many things for the first time—not just making them for the first time, but eating them for the first time, too! But in my free time, I started watching a little Food Network, and borrowing cookbooks from the library, and doing recipe exchanges with my friends. One of the big things every foodie learns is that a good cook can take almost any list of ingredients—regardless of the price—and turn them into something wonderful.

## PUT SOME STANDBYS ON YOUR MENU

In our house, Friday night means pizza for dinner—almost without fail. I instituted pizza night because this is such an economical meal, and because I can almost always make it from the ingredients we have on hand. What was simply a practical, cost-effective meal choice, however, has taken on a life of its own. My kids look forward to it every week. My husband and I enjoy the relaxed pizza-night vibe. My son, Ethan, recently asked if he could please invite a friend, explaining with a heavy heart that this boy had never had homemade pizza. Sometimes we switch things up a little—adding a different topping or, most recently, baking our new family favorite cheesy bread—but pizza night is always a hit.

Pizza Fridays are just one of a million ways to have an automatic fill-in on your meal calendar. Try instituting a soup-and-salad night, a slow-cooker chili day, taco night, or breakfast-for-dinner

## YOU DO THE MATH

### Pizza Night

Since I make my own pizza dough from bulk ingredients and homemade sauce, I actually only spend about five dollars on the makings of each Friday pizza night. If we ordered pizza each week instead of making it, we'd spend roughly twenty dollars, even with a coupon. I've been making pizza every Friday for five years: that's thirty-six hundred dollars in pizza savings—a lot of dough, if I do say so myself!

day (another favorite at our house). Whatever you choose, for every week, or every other week, you'll be able to keep the ingredients stocked up and be able to answer the all-important "what's for dinner?" for those days, without even giving it a second thought.

## THE BEST MOMADVICE

### Put Your Own Spin on It

Just because a meal is simple and inexpensive doesn't mean it can't be delicious, or festive, or a special occasion. If you want to make mealtimes more fun for your family, try a theme dinner. Think about the meal you are preparing, and add a decoration, an activity, or music to go with the theme. For example, at our house we all love Jazzy Sunday Brunch. I make waffles and cut up fruit, my husband puts on a Harry Connick Jr. CD, and we all eat late and read the Sunday paper together. It's not anything over the top, but every member of our family loves it. Try serving homemade sesame chicken with chopsticks instead of forks and knives, or hang a homemade paper lantern. Let your kids play waiter or waitress and serve you and your hubby a candlelit "night out," then do the same for them. Have a taco party, complete with salsa music and homemade maracas or a sombrero. The only limit is your imagination. When you find something that strikes a chord with your family, cycle it onto your meal calendar once in a while. My children each get to choose one day's dinner each time I make a new meal calendar. Some of their biggest favorites are meals where we enjoy not just the food but a creative spin on the evening as well.

## PREP YOUR PANTRY

A well-stocked pantry is like a magic cupboard for a good cook. You can truly find anything in there—or at least the ingredients to make anything. Since I make almost all my sauces, marinades, baking mixes, snacks, and treats myself, I keep a pantry that is heavy on the staples of our favorite meals. Many salad dressings and marinades call for the same basic ingredients—oil, vinegar, soy sauce, and so on. Every variety of canned tomato is a must. Pasta and rice, a few basic spices, and baking supplies are all staples as well.

I know that, like everything else, pantry products are subject to the family budget. However, if you keep a running list of what you've got and what you need, you can take advantage of every BOGO sale, deep discount from the Sunday flyer, or super coupon deal that comes along. Every cook needs to fine-tune her own pantry list to match the recipe box, but here's a list of the things I keep on hand for mine:

## TAKE FIVE

### Five "Magic" Meals

In every household there comes a day, not long before grocery shopping day, when it appears the cupboard is bare. In our house, it's the day when my husband looks into the fridge and the pantry and declares there is nothing to eat. Rather than loading into the car for groceries when this happens, I turn to a handful of menus we call "magic meals." Each earns its name because it can be made almost entirely of ingredients we always keep on hand in the pantry. These ingredients don't look like much when you glance around the kitchen cupboards, but the dishes you can whip up with them are all popular meals in our home, and they help me stretch my grocery budget when it appears we're at or near the end of the rations from my last shopping trip. You can find the recipes for each of these main dishes in chapter 3:

1. Homemade Pizza
2. Linguini with Clam Sauce
3. Spaghetti (usually with homemade meatballs from the freezer!)
4. Waffles
5. Tortellini Soup

Extra-virgin olive oil, canola oil, sesame oil

Balsamic vinegar, red wine vinegar, white wine vinegar

Flour, whole-wheat white flour, bread flour, cornmeal, salt, yeast

Sugar, confectioner's sugar, brown sugar

Baking soda, baking powder, cornstarch, cream of tartar, cinnamon

Pesto sauce, Worcestershire sauce, soy sauce, ketchup

Peanut butter, jelly, honey, syrup

Tomato sauce, crushed tomatoes, diced tomatoes, whole tomatoes, tomato paste

Pasta (linguine, spaghetti, bow ties, and shells), brown rice, white rice

Potatoes, canned pumpkin

Juice, coffee, tea, nonfat dairy creamer, evaporated milk, dry milk

Chicken broth, beef broth

Canned baby clams, tuna, salmon

Italian bread crumbs, panko bread crumbs, wheat germ, oatmeal, cereal

Semisweet chocolate, chocolate chips, cocoa powder, cake mixes, dried fruit

## FREEZE!

I know many frugal living advisors advocate using a big freezer to stock up on things like a side of beef, or a month's worth of frozen dinners, or even half a dozen gallons of milk. I've always been torn about this savings method, since I have some bad memories, both from my childhood and since I've been an adult, of having to throw away foods that have become freezer burned and ruined after sitting too long on ice.

I recommend a compromise—either a very well-organized and -utilized attached freezer or a half-chest freezer like the one we have in our home. Frozen foods are indeed very economical if they end up being put to good use. I recommend stocking frozen packages of chicken breasts and a basic white fish (we like tilapia), along with frozen vegetables and berries if you'll use them. We always pick blueberries in the summer, and I freeze them for year-round use in baked goods, sauces, and other recipes. If you have a garden, you may have other wonderful fresh fruits and veggies to store.

In addition to these standbys, I always try to keep a couple of frozen quick breads handy—you never know when you might need an impromptu snack or dessert. Lastly, I always keep an "emergency roast" in the freezer. If I run out of groceries, if we have company coming, if I need something slow-cooker friendly rather than stove-top-time-consuming, I thaw the roast and make my favorite Pot Roast Italiano or Slow-Cooked Italian Beef Sandwiches. If I don't use the roast over a couple of months, I just work it into my menu calendar and then replace it the next time I see a good sale.

## Make It Yourself

If someone had told my twenty-year-old self that she would one day shun almost all premade food products, brand-name groceries, and even most baking mixes, I would have laughed at the idea. The very thought of making the things that come so conveniently bottled and boxed at the market—bearing the friendly brand names I grew up with, no less—would have seemed ridiculous. Nevertheless, that's how things have turned out. The fact is that making almost everything from scratch saves my family a small fortune on groceries. Buying just the basic ingredients doesn't limit our meal choices, but it does save us the cost of everything from store-cooked products to premixed spice packages to the sky-high cost of packaging for things like sauces and salad dressings. Did you know packaging alone accounts for close to 10 percent of total food expenditures? Even though it's impossible to shop without buying any packaging at all, I choose not to pay that kind of percentage of our grocery bill for the privilege of getting all the glasses, cans, plastic tubs, cardboard boxes, and special pouches that come with many prepackaged and premixed foods. I can make all that stuff myself—and so can you.

I estimate that preparing almost everything homemade saves my family more than three hundred dollars a month. You might think that saving this way would cost too much time to be worth it, but I'm here to tell you I don't spend any more time working in my kitchen than most moms I know. Home cooking works amazingly well for me, both as a tool for running my frugal kitchen and as a means of feeding my family well.

## SAVE ON SAUCES

When I first started discovering how easy it is to make my own sauces, marinades, and salad dressings, I felt like I'd been let in on a big secret that had been kept from me all my life. The fact is, most of these things are so very simple to make—and for pennies on the dollar compared with prepackaged versions. I had no idea. I make my own barbecue sauce, enchilada sauce, honey-mustard sauce, Italian dressing, ranch dressing, and many others. I buy most of my sauce ingredients in bulk, to save even more on each batch. As an added benefit, homemade sauces don't contain all the dyes, preservatives, and other chemical ingredients found in their store-bought equivalents. They're simply better for you. You can find the recipes for many of my sauces in chapter 3.

## DIY MIXES

I'm the first to admit that even at this stage in my penny-pinching adventures, I still adore boxed cake mixes. I use them for all kinds of baked-goods recipes—not just cakes. They are one of my staple pantry ingredients, and I don't see that changing anytime soon. Aside from cake mix, though, I am an avid mix maker. I make my own bread mixes, pancake mixes, waffle mixes, seasoning mixes for everything from pumpkin pie to pot roast, soup mixes, and stuffing mixes. Did you know you can even make your own nondairy creamer? Your own pancake syrup? Your own sweetened condensed milk? Having an arsenal of recipes for make-it-yourself mixes not only can save you grocery dollars (not to mention crisis trips to the market when you find you're missing an ingredient), but they also make your pantry even more magical. After all, the more you can create from that cupboard, the less dependent you are on what's for sale and at what cost at the market.

## BUILD-YOUR-OWN SNACKS

If you've got kids, or a spouse, or a sweet tooth, or, well, a pulse, you've got to have snacks on hand pretty much all the time. These between-meal bites can be a budget killer if you're not careful. I know moms who easily spend more money on cookies, crackers, chips, and ice cream than they do on meats and vegetables—it's really far too easy to do.

In our house, I try to emphasize fresh fruit snacks whenever I can, and this has become a healthy habit for everyone in our family. However, I suspect no American family can live by fresh produce alone. I also make snacks once a week or so, and I always make extras so I can freeze them for a second showing at a later date. I make cookie bars and muffins, homemade slushes, and a shamelessly yummy knockoff of a Wendy's Frosty. I also make homemade chewy granola bars, which are so easy to prepare and healthy that I occasionally let my children have them for a quick breakfast. I individually wrap most of our snacks and keep them in a basket in the kitchen, so the kids can take them in lunches or on the go. I rarely buy prepackaged snacks at the market, and

## FAMILY TRADITIONS

### Our Own Coffee Shop

Here's a little secret I hate to admit: I'm a Starbucks junkie. That's right—the most expensive coffee I can find in my community is also one of my favorite things. This does not fit with my penny-pinching nature—nor with my image around town, since many members of our community know me from my segments on our local television station as the Frugal Mom. Anyone who knows me very well, though, would gladly tell you that I don't actually buy my Starbucks fix with cash money. I use gift cards. I receive them in return for all kinds of things I do for my friends and neighbors—taking family photos, knitting winter hats, running a few errands. One of my friends has threatened to have a T-shirt made up for me that says "Will Knit for Starbucks," and it would be all too true.

When the gift cards run out, however, I turn to my own recipes and kitchen tools to make my own gourmet brews. Fancy coffees are really a snap to make, and I love to re-create that coffee-shop experience at home with my family. I make cinnamon lattes, iced mochas, chai tea, and creative cocoas for my kids. We all enjoy the luxury of just sitting and sipping sometimes on chilly Indiana mornings, and I can get my coffee-shop-coffee fix anytime at all.

when I do, they make up a tiny percentage of my bill—the price of a rare treat rather than, as too often happens, a grocery "staple" that is expensive and moderately nutritious at best.

## RETHINK "FAST" FOOD

Every family can use the flexibility of an occasional fast-food meal—less stress, less prep, less cleanup: What's not to like? For many families, though, fast food means ordering in Chinese, which might run as much for a single delivery as I spend on three or four days' meals for my family; or going out for burgers, fries, and milkshakes with a similar result. While I love a day off cooking as much as the next mom, the version of fast food we've come to embrace is simply convenience foods I stock just for occasions when I haven't got the time, or the energy, to cook. In a pinch, I always have breaded chicken tenders or ravioli in the freezer, ready to pop on the stove or in the oven, ready to eat in ten or fifteen minutes. That's no longer than it would take to run to a fast-food place and get back home, but for a fraction of the cost.

# Smart Ways to Save Money and Time

If you're lucky, over time cooking becomes less of a chore and more of a habit—or better yet, a hobby. But whether you enjoy it or not, every homemaker benefits when we find a way to save time and energy in *any* part of the job—especially in cooking. I'm no efficiency expert, but I have paid very close attention to what meals, what tools, and what steps save me time slaving over a hot stove. The community of moms who come together at my website are also a wealth of great tips and ideas for getting well organized and getting things done with a minimum of fuss and mess. Here are some of my favorite ways to keep things simple in the kitchen.

## USE YOUR TOOLS

Kitchen gadgets seem to come in two varieties—the kind that sit in the cupboard taking up valuable space and those that actually make your life easier. I'm about as opposed to wasting money and space on the first kind as any mom on the planet, but there are a few kitchen gadgets I've found to be worth their weight in gold. These honored appliances save me hours each week in prep time and a big chunk of my grocery budget, too. Each has paid for itself many times over.

Here's a rundown on what each costs, what features matter, and the kinds of dishes they work for:

**Bread maker.** I use my bread maker two or three times every week—sometimes more. I recommend finding one in an online classified ad, at a garage sale, or used from a friend or neighbor rather than starting off with an expensive new one. Lots of people have these machines in a closet somewhere and never use them—and part of the reason is that commercial, pre-prepared bread mixes often cost as much as (or more than) a good loaf of bread from a bakery! Here's the thing, though: you don't have to buy bread mixes from the grocery store. I've never bought a single one. They are so very easy to make at home—not just basic bread, but also fancy herb-seasoned breads, sweet breakfast breads, cinnamon rolls, hamburger buns—even pitas and pizza dough. Most of these mixes cost pennies to make, and the results are delicious.

Since I use the bread maker a lot, I buy my ingredients in

bulk at a big-box store. I buy twenty-five-pound bags of bread flour and all-purpose flour, and I purchase yeast in bulk (never in those expensive little packets). I just dump all the ingredients in the machine in the morning and forget about it. I let some breads cook until they're ready to eat, and others—like my pizza crust—I prep as dough and bake later in the oven.

**Slow cooker.** Whenever possible, I like to start my family's dinner in the morning. Getting as much of the housework done in the first couple hours of the day as possible makes any homemaker's life easier, and if all the prep work for the evening's dinner can fit into that window, all the better. I believe the slow cooker can be every mom's best friend. What could be easier than throwing in a few ingredients, plugging it in, and then going about your day, without the worries of needing to figure out what everyone is going to eat for dinner? When I first started using a slow cooker to get meals on the table, I was really just trying to save myself the chaos of dinnertime meal prep after I had my second child. In the years since, though, I've discovered that this gadget is a priceless tool not just in saving time but in making delicious, richly flavored, clean-your-plate meals for my family.

At around twenty-five dollars new, a decent slow cooker is a bargain that will pay for itself in no time—I can't think of a better way to take inexpensive ingredients, especially humble cuts of meat, and turn them into wonderful family dinners. In our house, favorites like Pot Roast Italiano (served over orzo—yum!), Lemon Chicken, Italian Beef Sandwiches, Perfectly Pulled Pork Sandwiches, and Chicken Tacos are all family favorites. No matter what you make in the slow cooker, always make enough for leftovers. We have a couple of recipes that don't seem to yield much in the way of leftover servings no matter how much I make—but I love the fact that my husband and kids are so enthusiastic about some of my slow cooker meals that they always come back for seconds.

**Rice cooker.** Like the bread maker and the slow cooker, a rice cooker is all about the ability to pour in all the ingredients, push a couple of buttons, and forget about the whole deal until it's time for dinner. My rice cooker is a little luxury, because of course I can make rice on the stove as well as the next mom. At less than twenty dollars, though, this gadget has opened up a whole new world of side-dish possibilities for me. I make basic long-grain and brown rice, of course, but also tasty recipes for things like Lemon Rice Pilaf, Rice and Roni, and even fabulous risotto. Rice is just so darned cheap—if you can figure out new, tasty ways to prepare it for your family, you can serve side dishes for pennies per serving.

**Waffle maker.** In the world of high-value kitchen gadgets, the waffle maker may not be the biggest money saver or the most versatile, but in my book it definitely deserves a shout-out for being such a family-pleasing appliance. I'll be the first to admit that I only use my waffle maker once a week—usually on Sunday morning, to prepare our family's beloved Jazzy Sunday Brunch. That said, though, my little waffle-mongers (my darling children) eat waffles all week long, because I always make extras and pop them in the freezer for quick reheating. And though there are times when a perfectly prepared plain-and-simple waffle hits the spot, I also make a number of fancier versions, including Oatmeal Cookie Waffles and Whole-Wheat Cinnamon Waffles. In addition to making our own waffles, we sometimes make homemade syrups, too.

As with all my kitchen gadgets, my waffle maker is a basic

version that cost less than thirty dollars. I asked for it as a gift one year and have been having my own little wafflepalooza ever since. Waffles may be simple and inexpensive to make, but they inspire a level of enthusiasm and delight in my children that makes me feel like an all-star mom every time I crank out a new batch.

## TIME SAVER

### Have a Batch Day

If you get in the habit of using any of these kitchen gadgets, you can save yourself a ton of time by prepping multiple mix batches every time you need one. In our house, I enlist my children to help me, and we get all of our baking supplies, flavorings, and spices out at once, along with a box of resealable storage bags. Then we put together a couple dozen mixes for our favorite breads, waffles, and even rice mixes. The novelty of making a little assembly line and working together usually keeps everyone interested for the short time it takes to get the mixes ready. Once they're made, we label the bags and store them in the pantry. There's nothing easier than grabbing a ready-made mix from the pantry shelf when I want to make homemade bread or a quick batch of waffles—and it's great to know that by putting those mixes together ourselves, our family saved not only a small fortune on ingredients and packaging, but also exposure to countless preservatives and chemicals like MSG. We only have a batch day once every couple of months, and it takes just an hour or two to complete, but I love the self-sufficiency and time savings it gives our family.

## MAKE LOTS!

I'm a firm believer in prepping for more than one meal at a time. No matter what you're working on in the kitchen, it makes perfect sense to labor once with the goal of eating twice, three times, or even more. As long as you've got out all your ingredients and tools, and you're dirtying dishes and messing up your clean countertops anyway, make it worth your trouble! Here are a few suggestions:

**Dice twice.** You won't ever catch me cutting up vegetables for just a single meal. No matter what I'm making, I can always find a good use for an extra serving while the cutting board is out. Chop extra carrots, celery, and onions, for example, and store them in plastic containers in the fridge for soups, stews, and other slow cooker dishes.

This tactic saves even more time and trouble when you're planning grilled meals. Instead of prepping for a single cookout, why not get ready for a few at once? Buy your meat in bulk and double, or triple, your marinade recipe. If you are prepping chicken breasts, for example, divide a bulk package of meat into meal-sized portions, then chop it all into kebab-sized pieces. Toss the meat and your favorite marinade (teriyaki? Or maybe chicken Italiano?) into freezer-safe containers, then freeze your batches—meat, marinade, and all. The next time you want grilled chicken, you'll have your choice of well-seasoned, already-marinated, pre-prepared containers, ready to thaw and cook.

**Double everything.** Here's a motto to live by: Never make a single batch of meatballs! Or lasagna. Or cookies. Or anything, really. If you and your family enjoy a food, why not make more at once? I never put together a casserole without making two—one for the table, and one for the freezer. Ditto for baked goods. I always try to keep a batch of cookies, a special loaf of bread, or a casserole in a nice dish in the freezer so I have it handy if I want to share something with a friend or neighbor. And you really can get a lot of extra mileage out of making extra meatballs—not only is spaghetti with meatballs an almost universal hit, but they can also be used to make delicious hot meatball subs or thrown into a homemade soup, like my homemade California Italian Wedding Soup.

**Waste not.** There are so many kitchen resources that end up in the trash bin, or down the drain, or in the garbage disposal. Even those of us who take care to be frugal can easily overlook opportunities to save and store resources for later. Leftover coffee is a perfect example. Don't pour it down the drain! Pour any leftover coffee into an empty ice cube tray and freeze—you'll have the makings of fabulous, Starbucks-quality frozen mochas at your fingertips. Extra potatoes in almost any form are another great food to save. I always bake or mash extra potatoes and get a second meal out of the surplus. One of my family's favorites is meatloaf stuffed with garlic mashed potatoes. Another favorite is seasoned baked potato wedges—chopped and mixed with a little onion, bacon, and oil for delicious potato hash browns the second time around.

## PREP WITH PURPOSE

If you're going to be cooking, try to double or triple your efforts by making things simultaneously. For example, if I've already got the oven on for a roast chicken, I'll mix up a batch of cookies or granola bars for the week and put them in while it's still hot. If a recipe calls for boiled pasta, you can bet we'll be having boiled or steamed veggies on the side, because I can steam them on a splatter guard over the pasta, or just toss them in with the noodles for the last couple of minutes to give them a quick blanch. Likewise, if we're having roasted meat, we're having roasted veggies, too—tossed with olive oil and sprinkled with garlic salt or lemon pepper—yum.

........................

For most families, achieving peace and love within the budget begins not just at home, but in the kitchen. This is the place where you can both save and share, pinch pennies and show love. It is the heart of our family's frugal, happy home, and I hope yours is a happy place in your family life, too.

# 3

........

# Recipes to Prepare and Share

## HOMEMADE SPICE AND EASY-PREP MIXES

### HOMEMADE POULTRY SEASONING MIX

2 teaspoons ground sage

1½ teaspoons ground thyme

1 teaspoon ground marjoram

¾ teaspoon ground rosemary

½ teaspoon nutmeg

½ teaspoon finely ground black pepper

Mix all ingredients well. Store in an airtight container.

## HOMEMADE RICE SEASONING MIX

¾ cup chicken bouillon granules
½ cup dried parsley
1 tablespoon basil
1 tablespoon dill weed
2 tablespoons dried onion flakes
1 teaspoon seasoning salt
2 teaspoons garlic powder
1 teaspoon lemon pepper seasoning
1 cup almonds, coarsely chopped (optional)

Mix together and store in an airtight container. When preparing rice, bring 2 cups water to a boil and add 1 cup rice and 3 tablespoons seasoning. Reduce to simmer and cook for 18 minutes.

## HOMEMADE BAKING MIX
## (SUBSTITUTE FOR BISQUICK)

5½ cups sifted flour
1 teaspoon baking soda
3 tablespoons baking powder
1 cup shortening

Mix all ingredients well until crumbly. Store in an airtight container.

## HOMEMADE ITALIAN DRESSING
## SEASONING MIX

1½ teaspoons garlic powder

1 tablespoon onion powder

2 tablespoons ground oregano

1 tablespoon dried parsley

1 tablespoon granulated sugar

2 tablespoons salt (adjust to your own personal preference)

1 teaspoon black pepper

1 teaspoon ground basil

¼ teaspoon ground thyme

½ teaspoon dried celery flakes

Mix all ingredients together and store in an airtight container. To prepare the dressing: Mix 2 tablespoons of the mix with ¼ cup vinegar, 2 tablespoons of water, and ½ to ⅔ cup olive oil or canola oil.

## HOMEMADE RANCH DRESSING MIX

½ cup dry buttermilk

1 tablespoon dried parsley, crushed

1 teaspoon dried dill weed

1 teaspoon onion powder

1 teaspoon dried onion flakes

1 teaspoon salt

½ teaspoon garlic powder

¼ teaspoon ground pepper

Combine all ingredients in a food processor and grind until it becomes a fine powder. Store in an airtight container. To prepare the dressing: Combine 1 tablespoon mix with 1 cup mayonnaise and 1 cup milk.

## HOMEMADE CROUTONS

*If you have never made homemade croutons before, you are missing out. Be sure to check if your favorite sandwich shops or bakers sell day-old bread. Stale bread is perfect for this project.*

6 slices of bread (any kind)
1 teaspoon basil
1 teaspoon oregano
Liberal sprinkling of garlic salt (to taste)
¼ cup olive oil

Preheat oven to 350 degrees. Cube bread into desired size and toss into a bowl. Sprinkle all of the seasonings on top of your bread cubes. Drizzle olive oil over the cubes and then toss gently with your fingers. When all pieces have been coated, put cubes into a single layer on a cookie sheet. Bake for 20 minutes. Allow to cool. Place in an airtight container. These can be stored for up to 4 weeks.

# MAKE-YOUR-OWN "STOVE TOP" STUFFING

6 cups cubed bread
1 tablespoon parsley flakes
3 tablespoons chicken bouillon powder
¼ cup dried minced onion
½ cup dried minced celery (or fresh celery may be sautéed
    and added just before cooking)
1 teaspoon thyme
1 teaspoon pepper
½ teaspoon sage
⅓ teaspoon salt

Preheat the oven to 350 degrees. Spread the cubes on a cookie sheet and bake for 8 to 10 minutes, turning to brown evenly. Cool. In a plastic bag or bowl, toss the cubes with the rest of the ingredients until well coated. Store in a tightly closed container in the pantry for up to 4 months, or in the freezer for up to a year. To use: Combine 2 cups stuffing mix with ½ cup water and 2 tablespoons melted butter. Stir to combine thoroughly. Warm on the stove or in a microwave. Stir again just before serving. Makes 4 servings.

## APPETIZERS

### MAKE-AHEAD SPINACH BALLS

*This fast little appetizer is perfect to keep on hand in your fridge for a fun, savory snack that is sure to satisfy! Even if you're not a spinach lover, the stuffing mix takes away from the spinach flavor, making this a more savory dish than you might expect. These are the perfect poppers to serve while enjoying a few board games around the kitchen table.*

2 (10-ounce) packages frozen spinach
1 package chicken-flavored stuffing mix
1 cup grated Parmesan cheese
6 eggs, lightly beaten
¾ cup butter, melted
Salt and pepper to taste

Preheat oven to 350 degrees. Cook spinach according to instructions and drain in a sieve. Use the back of a wooden spoon to press the spinach against the sieve to remove as much moisture as possible. In a bowl, combine the spinach, stuffing mix, cheese, eggs, butter, salt, and pepper. Mix thoroughly and roll into small balls ¾ to 1 inch in size. Place on a cookie sheet. Bake for 7 to 10 minutes. Serve hot. Makes 6 servings.

### SPUNKY SPINACH DIP

*You can never go wrong with a good spinach dip, and this one is my absolute favorite because of the unexpected flavor that the salsa adds. You can make it as mild or as spicy as you like. I opt for a mild salsa and serve it with pita chips, tortilla chips, or fresh veggies for a little lighter fare.*

2 cups salsa (approximately one standard-size jar)
2 cups Monterey Jack cheese
8 ounces low-fat or fat-free cream cheese, softened and cubed
10 ounces frozen chopped spinach (thawed and drained)

Combine ingredients together in a mixing bowl. Place in an oven-safe dish and bake, covered, at 350 degrees for 20 to 25 minutes (double your cooking time for a double batch). Serve with your favorite dipping crackers, pita chips, or cold veggies. Makes approximately 3 cups dip.

## BACON AND RANCH CHEESE BALL

*This cheese ball is so embarrassingly easy, but is always a showstopper when I bring it to holiday get-togethers. Put the ingredients for this recipe on your grocery list and relish both the ease of its preparation and the compliments it inspires!*

2 (8-ounce) packages of low-fat cream cheese, softened
1 package ranch dressing mix
1½ cups shredded cheddar cheese, divided
5 to 7 strips bacon, cooked and crumbled (or buy prepackaged crumbled bacon)

Mix all of the ingredients except ½ cup cheddar cheese together with a mixer until they are incorporated. Mold into a ball and wrap in plastic wrap to store. When ready to serve, roll the cheese ball in the remaining ½ cup cheese to coat. Serve with assorted crackers. Makes 1 ball, enough to serve 8 as an appetizer.

## CHOCOLATE CHIP COOKIE DOUGH DIP

8 ounces cream cheese, softened
½ cup unsalted butter, softened
¼ teaspoon vanilla extract
¾ cup powdered sugar
2 tablespoons brown sugar
¾ cup miniature semisweet chocolate chips
More chocolate chips (optional) or chopped nuts, to sprinkle
    on top

In a mixing bowl, beat cream cheese, butter, and vanilla until fluffy. Gradually add sugars and beat until just combined. Stir in chocolate chips. Transfer to a serving dish, cover, and refrigerate for 2 hours. Just before serving, top with additional chocolate chips or chopped nuts. Serve with graham crackers or chocolate animal crackers. Makes enough to serve 8 as an appetizer.

## SOUPS

### HOMEMADE ONION SOUP MIX

¾ cup instant minced onion

4 teaspoons onion powder

⅓ cup beef-flavored bouillon powder

¼ teaspoon celery seed, crushed

¼ teaspoon sugar

Mix all the ingredients and store in an airtight container. To use, combine 2 tablespoons mix to 1 cup boiling water. Cover and simmer for 15 minutes. Makes about 8 (1-cup) servings.

### HOMEMADE CONDENSED CREAM OF CHICKEN SOUP

1½ cups chicken broth

½ teaspoon poultry seasoning

¼ teaspoon onion powder

¼ teaspoon garlic powder

⅓ teaspoon salt

¼ teaspoon parsley

Dash of paprika

1½ cups milk, divided

¾ cup flour

In a medium-sized saucepan, boil chicken broth, the seasonings, and ½ cup of the milk for 1 or 2 minutes. In a bowl, whisk together the remaining 1 cup of milk and the flour. Add to boiling mixture and continue whisking briskly until the mixture boils and thickens. Makes 4 servings.

## HOMEMADE TOMATO SOUP

*Skip the canned tomato soup and opt for a satisfying bowl of homemade soup made from a few simple pantry ingredients. This tomato soup has all of our favorite flavors in the perfect combination for our family. Once you make this soup, you'll never buy canned tomato soup again.*

2 cloves garlic, minced
2 tablespoons olive oil
2 (28-ounce) cans crushed tomatoes
1 (28-ounce) can whole tomatoes
3 cups chicken or vegetable stock
2 teaspoons kosher salt
2 teaspoons sugar
¼ cup jarred pesto
½ cup heavy cream

In a large pot, sauté the garlic in the olive oil over medium heat for 1 minute. Add crushed tomatoes and the whole tomatoes (including their juices). Use your wooden spoon to break the whole tomatoes apart into the crushed tomatoes. Add your chicken or vegetable stock, salt, sugar, and pesto. Let this simmer for 15 minutes. Turn your heat to low and then add the heavy cream. Garnish the soup with homemade croutons (see recipe above) and Parmesan cheese. Makes 4 servings.

# PESTO CHICKEN TORTELLINI SOUP

*This is a really yummy, hearty soup—suitable for a meal with a small salad and a loaf of bread. When reheating, feel free to add some additional chicken broth to thin the soup, as the tortellini will absorb some liquid.*

2 cloves garlic, minced
2 tablespoons olive oil
2 (14.5-ounce) cans petite diced tomatoes
8 cups chicken broth
1 pound chicken herb tortellini or tortellini of your choice
    (I use the refrigerated kind, but you can also use
    dried pasta)
9 ounces spinach, chopped
¼ cup basil pesto
Parmesan cheese, for garnish

In a large pot, sauté the garlic in the olive oil. After a minute or so, add the diced tomatoes and chicken broth. Bring the broth to a rolling boil and then add your tortellini. Cook tortellini as directed on package. In the last minute of cooking time, mix in the chopped spinach and stir in the ¼ cup of basil pesto. Ladle into bowls and sprinkle with Parmesan cheese. Makes 6 servings.

## QUICK CHICKEN NOODLE SOUP

*This is the kind of chicken soup Grandma used to make—friends who have tasted it can't believe how completely different this easy home-made soup is from the canned variety.*

2 to 3 cups egg noodles (I like the Reames brand in the
    frozen foods section)
2 tablespoons olive oil
2 stalks chopped celery
3 chopped carrots
12 cups low-sodium chicken broth
1 rotisserie or home-roasted chicken
⅓ cup cornstarch
¼ cup water
Salt and pepper to taste
Fresh parsley, for garnish

Bring a large pot of lightly salted water to a boil. Add egg noodles and cook until tender. Drain and rinse under cool running water. Meanwhile, heat olive oil in a large saucepan or Dutch oven and sauté the celery and carrots for 5 minutes to start your soup base (or you can skip this step and proceed as directed, if you like crunchier vegetables). Use the large pot from the pasta to heat up the chicken broth and bring it to a simmer. Stir in celery and carrots. Gently add your whole rotisserie chicken and all of the drippings from the pan and put a lid on the pot. Reduce heat, cover, and simmer 15 minutes. In a small bowl, mix cornstarch and water together until cornstarch is completely dissolved. Pull out your chicken and dice it. Gradually add the cornstarch to the soup, stirring constantly. Stir in noodles and diced chicken and heat through. Add salt and pepper to taste. Toss in a handful of fresh chopped parsley and serve immediately. Makes 8 servings.

## GREEK LEMON CHICKEN SOUP

*This soup . . . oh, this soup. Words seem inadequate to explain how it tastes: a little like love, comfort, and coming home. If ever there was a soup that a girl could be proud of, this is mine. It is rich and creamy tasting, but lightened with lemon. It is, in my humble opinion, the best pot of soup I have ever made.*

1 cup orzo pasta
4 carrots, chopped
2 tablespoons olive oil (optional)
8 cups chicken broth
½ cup fresh lemon juice
Diced, cooked chicken meat (from a rotisserie chicken)
3 egg yolks
Lemon slices, fresh parsley, salt, and pepper for seasoning
    and garnish

Bring a large pot of lightly salted water to a boil. Add orzo noodles and cook until tender. Drain, and rinse under cool running water. Meanwhile, in a large saucepan or Dutch oven, sauté the carrots in two tablespoons of olive oil for five minutes to start your soup base, or you can skip this step and proceed as directed, if you desire a crunchier vegetable. Use your large pasta pot to heat up the broth and fresh lemon juice and bring to a simmer. Gently add the carrots, diced chicken, and any drippings, and put a lid on your pot. Reduce heat, cover, and simmer 15 minutes.

Meanwhile, beat the egg yolks until light in color. Gradually add some of the hot soup to the egg yolks, stirring constantly. Return the egg mixture to the soup pot and heat through. Add the orzo. Season to taste, and toss in a handful of fresh chopped parsley. Ladle hot soup into bowls and garnish with lemon slices. Makes 4 to 6 servings.

## CALIFORNIA ITALIAN WEDDING SOUP

*Keep your freezer stocked with packages of prepared meatballs to save you time in the kitchen. With frozen meatballs, you can make this soup on a moment's notice for a friend or family member in need.*

1 cup pasta (preferably orzo or small shells)
2 tablespoons olive oil
3 to 4 carrots, chopped into uniform pieces
2 cloves garlic, minced
8 cups low-sodium chicken broth
1 can (2 cups) beef broth
1 lemon, zested and juiced (save the juice for finishing
    the dish)
1 pound of prepared meatballs
2 tablespoons freshly chopped basil
2 cups fresh baby spinach
Parmesan cheese (optional, for garnish)

Bring a large pot of lightly salted water to a boil. Add pasta and cook until tender. Drain and rinse under cool running water. Heat the olive oil in a large saucepan or Dutch oven and sauté the carrots for 5 minutes. Add the minced garlic and cook for 1 minute (being careful to not allow the garlic to burn). Heat the broth (chicken and beef) and add the lemon zest, allowing the broth to simmer. Gently add your cooked meatballs to the pot. Reduce heat and cook until the meatballs are heated through. Toss in a handful of fresh chopped basil, the lemon juice, and fresh spinach. Let simmer 5 minutes, then ladle into bowls and sprinkle with Parmesan cheese. Makes 6 servings.

## BAKED POTATO SOUP

*This delicious, stick-to-your-ribs soup makes a fantastic fix-ahead lunch or dinner on a cold winter day. Adults and kids alike love the creamy, cheesy texture and flavor.*

4 large baked potatoes (make extras every time you bake
   them for recipes like this!)
⅔ cup butter
⅔ cup flour
6 cups milk (whole or 2 percent)
¾ teaspoon salt
½ teaspoon pepper
2 cups shredded cheese, divided
1 cup (8 ounces) sour cream
12 slices bacon, fried and crumbled

Cut potatoes in half. Scoop out the pulp and put it in a small bowl. Melt butter in a large pot. Add flour. Gradually stir in milk. Continue to stir until smooth, thickened, and bubbly. Stir in potato pulp, salt and pepper, and ¾ of the cheese. Cook until heated. Stir in sour cream. Top with remaining bacon and cheese. Makes 6 servings.

# ITALIAN VEGGIE AND PASTA SOUP

½ pound ground turkey

3 carrots, chopped very small

4 stalks celery

2 cans diced tomatoes (do not drain)

2 cans red kidney beans, drained

3 cans beef broth

1 jar spaghetti sauce

8 ounces pasta (your choice, but elbow macaroni works
    great)

Brown the ground turkey in a skillet. Drain fat and place turkey in the slow cooker. Add all of the ingredients except the pasta to the cooker. Cook soup on low for 7 to 8 hours or on high for 4 to 5 hours. During the last 30 minutes (if on high) or 1 hour (on low) add the pasta. Serve with a loaf of crusty bread and cold veggies. Makes 8 servings.

*Note*: If you plan to freeze the soup for leftovers, cook the pasta separately. When serving the soup, ladle in the pasta and then pour the soup on top. The pasta absorbs liquid and will not freeze as well as the rest of the soup. You can make a fresh pot of pasta when you thaw the soup for another night and it will taste as fresh as the day that you made it.

## MAIN DISHES: CHICKEN

## CHICKEN BROCCOLI LO MEIN

*I make hot tea and buy a package of fortune cookies when I make this recipe, and my kids love the cheap thrill of the dining adventure at home. I'm always looking for ways to help my children enjoy vegetables. The trick with broccoli seems to be to never serve it too soft. I guess kids just like crunchy stuff! Boiling it in the salted pasta water for 4 minutes for this recipe makes it just the right bright green and crisp to be a hit at our house.*

1 pound linguine
2 broccoli crowns, cut into bite-size pieces
2 cups fresh mushrooms
2 tablespoons vegetable oil
1½ pounds boneless, skinless chicken breasts
6 tablespoons soy sauce
2 tablespoons white vinegar
2 tablespoons ketchup
1 ladle (about ½ cup) salted pasta water

Cook pasta as directed. Add cut broccoli to boiling pasta and water for the last 4 minutes of cooking, then remove from heat and set aside. Clean and chop mushrooms. Heat oil. Cut chicken into bite-size pieces. When all the chicken is cut, add it to the skillet. Add mushrooms to the skillet. Cook for 5 to 6 minutes or until mushrooms have released their liquid and chicken is cooked through. Add soy sauce, vinegar, and ketchup. Stir to combine. Add cooked pasta and broccoli and serve immediately. Makes 4 servings.

## CHICKEN TACOS (SLOW COOKER)

*These 3-ingredient slow cooker chicken tacos are a great weeknight meal when your calendar is booked with extracurricular activities. Serve with all your favorite taco toppings and tortilla chips for an easy meal.*

1 taco seasoning packet (brand of your choice)
1 cup chicken broth
1 pound boneless, skinless chicken breasts

Dissolve taco seasoning into chicken broth. Place chicken breasts in slow cooker and pour broth over them. Cook on low setting for 6 hours. With 2 forks, shred the chicken meat into bite-size pieces. Makes 4 servings.

## STICKY CHICKEN (SLOW COOKER)

*This is my new favorite chicken. To me, it tastes like a rotisserie chicken (without the price tag!) because it has that slow-cooked flavor. If you want the chicken to retain its shape in the cooker, rest the chicken on a rack or 3 small aluminum foil "pedestals" so it will not be resting in its own juices. If you want to crisp the skin, the oven can act like a slow cooker when the bird is roasted at 250 degrees for 4 hours uncovered. Use any leftover chicken to throw on a salad for the next day's lunch.*

1 tablespoon salt
2 teaspoons paprika

2 teaspoons dried oregano leaves

2 teaspoons dried thyme leaves

1 teaspoon pepper

1 teaspoon garlic salt

3-pound roasting chicken

1 cup chopped onion

In a small bowl, combine all ingredients except chicken and onion. Rub herb mixture inside and outside of chicken. Place in a food storage bag; seal bag. Refrigerate overnight. Remove chicken from bag; stuff with onion. Place in slow cooker on low for 6 to 8 hours or high for 2 to 4 hours. Chicken is done when juices run clear and chicken reaches 180 degrees. Let stand 15 minutes before carving. Makes 4 servings.

## BBQ CHICKEN (SLOW COOKER)

2 cups ketchup

4 tablespoons brown sugar

1 tablespoon Worcestershire sauce

1 tablespoon soy sauce

1 tablespoon vinegar

½ teaspoon garlic powder

4 chicken breasts

Toasted buns

Mix together all ingredients except chicken in slow cooker. Add the chicken, coating each piece in sauce. Cook on high for 4 hours. Remove chicken and shred with 2 forks. Return to pot and stir in sauce to coat. Serve on toasted buns. Makes 4 servings.

*Note:* The leftovers can be frozen and reheated for sandwiches or can be used for BBQ pizzas. You can purchase a prepared crust to save yourself some time. Cover the crust with the leftover BBQ chicken and then top with mozzarella cheese.

## LEMON CHICKEN (SLOW COOKER)

*If you are looking for an elegant dinner made in your slow cooker, this is the meal. I love to serve this with a side of rice and loaf of crusty bread.*

3-pound broiler-fryer chicken, whole or pieces
Salt and pepper to taste
1 teaspoon dried oregano
½ teaspoon dried rosemary
2 cloves garlic, minced
2 tablespoons butter
¼ cup sherry wine or chicken broth
¼ cup lemon juice

Wash chicken, pat dry, and season generously with salt and pepper; sprinkle half of the oregano, rosemary, and garlic inside the cavity of the chicken. Melt the butter in a frying pan and brown the chicken, then transfer to slow cooker and sprinkle with remaining oregano, rosemary, and garlic. Add sherry or broth to frying pan and stir to loosen brown bits; pour into slow cooker. Cover, cook on low for 7 hours. Add lemon juice and cook 1 more hour (total of 8). Transfer chicken to cutting board; skim fat from juices and serve juices over chicken. Makes 4 servings.

## CHICKEN ITALIANO

*When I was growing up, my mom used to buy a product called Chicken Tonight that had a sauce that you could cook your chicken in to make a fast dinner. My mom served it over rice as a quick weeknight meal, and it was always a favorite of mine. This recipe reminds me a lot of that dish and is equally easy to prepare. You can throw it in your slow cooker or you can put it in the oven for last-minute guests.*

4 chicken breasts
2 cups spaghetti sauce
⅓ cup chopped tomatoes (you can use fresh or a can of
    diced tomatoes)
½ cup Italian dressing

Place all ingredients in your slow cooker. Cover and cook on low for 6 hours. Serve over spaghetti or rice with a sprinkle of Parmesan cheese. Makes 4 servings.

# ROSEMARY RANCH CHICKEN KABOBS

*If you are struggling with getting chicken that is perfectly cooked on the grill, then I highly recommend trying these kabobs. This chicken is moist and delicious, and cooking kabobs is a lot easier than trying to figure out if an entire chicken breast is done or not.*

½ cup olive oil
½ cup ranch dressing
3 tablespoons Worcestershire sauce
1 teaspoon dried rosemary
2 teaspoons salt
2 teaspoons lemon juice
1 teaspoon white vinegar
5 skinless, boneless chicken breast halves—cut into 1-inch cubes

In a medium bowl, stir together the olive oil, ranch dressing, Worcestershire sauce, rosemary, salt, lemon juice, and white vinegar. Let stand for 5 minutes. Place chicken in the bowl, and stir to coat with the marinade. Cover and refrigerate for 30 minutes. Preheat the grill for medium-high heat. Thread chicken onto skewers and discard marinade. Lightly oil the grill grate. Grill skewers for 8 to 12 minutes, or until the chicken is no longer pink in the center and the juices run clear. Makes 5 servings.

# CRISPY BAKED CHICKEN TENDERS

*These chicken tenders are the perfect weeknight meal, and my kids love these just as much as those fast-food chicken nuggets that we would get in the drive-thru. Save the leftovers for tortilla wraps or for salad topping for easy lunches.*

2 cups panko bread crumbs (in the international aisle or by
    the baking aisle of your grocery store)
2 tablespoons olive oil
¼ cup Parmesan cheese
½ cup all-purpose flour
1 teaspoon garlic powder
1 teaspoon salt
¼ teaspoon cayenne pepper
3 large egg whites
1 tablespoon water
1 tablespoon Dijon mustard
1 teaspoon minced fresh thyme or ¼ teaspoon dried
Cooking spray
1½ pounds boneless chicken tenderloins

Preheat the oven to 475 degrees. In a shallow dish, mix together the panko bread crumbs, oil, and Parmesan cheese. In a second shallow dish, whisk together the flour, garlic powder, salt, and cayenne pepper. In a bowl, whisk together the egg whites, water, mustard, and thyme. Spray a wire rack lightly with cooking spray and place over a rimmed baking sheet. Working in batches, dredge a few pieces of the chicken in the flour, then the egg whites, and finally the bread crumbs to coat, shaking off the excess between each step. Lay the coated pieces on the prepared wire rack and repeat with the remaining chicken. Spray the tops of the chicken pieces lightly with the cooking spray. Bake until the chicken is cooked through, 10 to 12 minutes. Makes 4 to 6 servings.

## CHICKEN PESTO OPEN-FACED FLATBREAD SANDWICH

*This recipe has become my new weeknight go-to recipe for a quick, easy, and flavorful meal. The only problem in our house is when we run out of ingredients to make these. Once you try these, I know that you will agree.*

½ cup jarred pesto
1 tablespoon balsamic vinegar
½ teaspoon salt
4 pieces flatbread
1 cup Italian blend shredded cheese
1 pound diced grilled chicken
Lettuce
Tomatoes

In a jar, mix together the pesto, balsamic vinegar, and salt. Set aside. Turn your oven's broiler to high. On a cookie sheet, top individual flatbreads with a handful of shredded Italian cheese (approximately ¼ cup each). Broil the flatbread for 2 minutes, or until cheese is melted. Top each flatbread with grilled chicken, lettuce, and fresh tomato slices. Finish each flatbread off with a generous dollop of your pesto drizzle. Makes 4 sandwiches.

## MAIN DISHES: PORK

### RANCH PORK CHOPS

*This simple method of dredging pork chops in flour, dressing, and topping with cheese doesn't yield the prettiest chops, but it definitely is our favorite go-to recipe for pork chops. You won't believe how good these smell in the oven. Served with brown rice and veggies, they make a wonderfully fast weeknight meal.*

¼ cup flour
1 teaspoon dried Italian seasoning
½ cup ranch dressing
4 to 6 pork chops (I purchase the center cut and not the assorted variety)
½ cup Parmesan cheese

Preheat oven to 375 degrees. In a shallow container, mix together the flour and Italian seasonings. In another shallow container, pour in the ranch dressing. Trim all fat from the pork chops and then dredge in the flour. Dip the pork chop into the dressing on both sides. Place pork chops on a greased baking dish and sprinkle the tops with a little Parmesan cheese. Bake for 35 minutes. Makes 4 to 6 servings.

# PERFECTLY PULLED PORK SANDWICHES

*I love to buy a 2-liter bottle of root beer for this recipe and serve my kids an old-fashioned root beer float for a special treat with their sandwiches. It has become a pulled pork sandwich tradition in our house!*

1 (4-pound) Boston butt (or pork shoulder)
1 (12-fluid-ounce) can or bottle of root beer
1 (18-ounce) bottle of your favorite barbecue sauce (we love Sweet Baby Ray's Barbecue Sauce)
6 hamburger buns, split and lightly toasted

Place the pork meat in a slow cooker; pour the root beer over the meat. Cover and cook on low until well cooked and the pork shreds easily (I cook for 8 hours). Shred the meat and drain the root beer from the slow cooker. Stir in barbecue sauce and toss gently. Serve meat in your favorite hamburger bun. Makes 6 servings.

# SIMPLY DELICIOUS APPLE PORK CHOPS

*Looking for ways to use up those extra apples in your fruit bowl? Look no further! These simple apple pork chops happen to be one of my favorite fall recipes!*

1 tablespoon olive oil
4 pork chops (½ inch thick)
½ teaspoon salt
Ground black pepper
3 tablespoons brown sugar
½ teaspoon ground cinnamon
¼ cup apple juice
2 apples, peeled, cored, and sliced (I use Granny
    Smith apples)

Preheat oven to 375 degrees. Heat oil in large skillet. Brown the pork chops on both sides. Place chops in a baking dish just large enough so they do not overlap and sprinkle them with salt and pepper. In a small bowl, combine the brown sugar, cinnamon, apple juice, and apples. Give them a toss together. Pour the mixture over the chops. Cover and bake in the preheated oven for 30 to 45 minutes. Makes 4 servings.

# PARMESAN SAGE–CRUSTED PORK CHOPS

*These pork chops are restaurant worthy and made my family fall in love with pork chops. The lemon zest in the breading adds a lot of flavor, and these are fabulous served with your favorite buttered noodles.*

2 cups Italian bread crumbs

1 cup grated Parmesan cheese

1 tablespoon sage (dried)

1 teaspoon grated lemon peel (save the lemons for
   squeezing over the hot chops)

¼ cup flour, seasoned with salt and pepper

4 pork chops, about 1 inch thick (you can use bone-in or
   -out ones)

2 large eggs, whisked

⅛ to ¼ cup butter

2 tablespoons olive oil

Sprinkle of fresh parsley

Preheat oven to 425 degrees. In a medium bowl, mix bread crumbs, grated Parmesan cheese, dried sage, and grated lemon peel. Put flour seasoned with salt and pepper on a plate; coat chops with flour. Dip in egg. Then dip in bread crumb mixture. Melt butter and olive oil in an oven-proof skillet. Brown chops until golden. Transfer to oven and bake until meat thermometer says 150 degrees, about 20 minutes. Makes 4 servings.

# CLASSIC PORK CHOPS (SLOW COOKER)

*This recipe is so simple, and simply wonderful. The first time I served it at our house, my husband didn't even believe it was pork chops, because the meat was so tender!*

4 pork chops (approximately 3 pounds)
1 package onion soup mix
1 cup reduced-sodium chicken broth

Place pork chops in slow cooker. In a separate bowl, combine soup mix and chicken broth and stir. Pour over chops. Cook on low heat for 6 to 8 hours. Makes 4 servings.

## MAIN DISHES: BEEF

## POT ROAST ITALIANO (SLOW COOKER)

*I serve Pot Roast Italiano over orzo to dress it up a bit. This recipe is so basic, but the rich sauce and the tender beef make a fabulous dinner. My kids love this one; my husband loves it; dinner guests ask for the recipe. It's one of the staple meals I come back to again and again.*

2 medium onions, sliced
3 pounds beef chuck roast
Salt and pepper to taste
1 can diced tomatoes, drained
1 (12-ounce) can tomato sauce
2 tablespoons red wine vinegar
1 teaspoon oregano
1 teaspoon garlic powder
1 teaspoon basil
1 (6-ounce) can tomato paste
Grated Parmesan cheese

Place sliced onions on bottom of slow cooker. Place roast on onions. Season with salt and pepper. Pour diced tomatoes, tomato sauce, vinegar, and spices over roast. Cook on high for 1 hour, and then low for 8 hours. Transfer meat to cutting board and cut into chunks. Meanwhile, whisk tomato paste into the gravy in the cooker and add Parmesan cheese to taste. Gravy will get thicker after 1 or 2 minutes. Add meat back to gravy and serve. Makes 6 servings.

## ITALIAN BEEF SANDWICHES
## (SLOW COOKER)

*I served this to my sister-in-law, who stated, "I want to drink the juice—it is so good!" This is perfect for any of your family gatherings or potlucks. Buy the cheapest cut of meat possible for this dish. The meat will cook a long time, and the slow cooker will tenderize even the toughest cuts. Use a slotted spoon to serve meat on large buns or rolls to keep the juice from making buns soggy. Serve the juice in a small ramekin, on the side, for dipping your sandwich. If you like a tangier beef, load up your slow cooker with more red wine vinegar and Worcestershire sauce (to taste).*

1 (5-pound) roast
3 cups water
1 teaspoon salt
1 teaspoon pepper
1 teaspoon oregano
1 teaspoon basil
1 teaspoon onion powder
½ teaspoon garlic powder
1 package Italian salad dressing
¼ cup red wine vinegar
1 tablespoon Worcestershire sauce

Trim excess fat from roast. Place roast in the slow cooker. Mix water with all seasonings and dressing and pour over roast. Mix vinegar and Worcestershire and pour over all. Cover and cook on low 8 to 10 hours. Remove meat, allow to cool slightly, then shred, discarding any fat. Return shredded meat to broth in the slow cooker and cook on high until heated through, 15 to 30 minutes. Makes 8 servings.

## TO-DIE-FOR POT ROAST

*This is the best roast ever. It is a challenge, in our house, to have any left over. If you want to add to the color of the meat, sear it in a pan before placing into the slow cooker. If you'd like to make this a 1-dish affair, just add carrots and potatoes to the cooker with the roast, and you'll have everything ready at once.*

1 (4-pound) beef roast, any kind
1 package dried brown gravy mix
1 package dried Italian salad dressing mix
1 package dried ranch dressing mix
1 cup water

Place beef roast in slow cooker. Combine the dried mixes together in a bowl and sprinkle over the roast. Pour the water around the roast. Cook on low for 7 to 9 hours. Makes 6 to 8 servings.

# SLOPPY JOES

1 pound ground beef

1 cup chopped onions (I omit these because I don't like onions)

1 cup ketchup

1 tablespoon mustard

2 tablespoons red wine vinegar

1 teaspoon salt

2 teaspoons Worcestershire sauce

In a large skillet, brown beef with onions (make sure to drain or rinse your meat after this step). Mix the rest of the ingredients together. Add to beef and onions. Cook for 1 hour over medium heat, stirring occasionally. Serve on warm hamburger buns. Makes 4 servings.

*Note:* For a creative alternative to the regular old Sloppy Joe, why not make Sloppy Joe Turnovers out of the leftover meat? Buy a tube of biscuits and roll each biscuit out into a 4-inch round. Place ¼ cup of the meat mixture in the center of each round and fold over the top. Seal edges firmly with a fork and bake for 15 minutes at 375 degrees. It is a great way to get children to eat their meat because, well, what kid doesn't love any food that comes in a pocket?

# GRILLED GROUND BEEF GYROS

## Sauce

    1 (8-ounce) container plain yogurt

    ⅓ cup chopped seeded cucumber

    2 cloves garlic, minced

    1 teaspoon sugar

## Filling

    1 pound lean ground beef (or you can use ground turkey)

    2 teaspoons dried oregano

    1 teaspoon garlic powder

    1 teaspoon onion powder

    1 teaspoon salt

    ¾ teaspoon pepper

    4 pita breads (store-bought or you can try my easy bread
        machine pita)

    2 cups shredded lettuce

    1 large tomato, chopped

    1 small onion, chopped

In a bowl, combine first 4 ingredients to make the sauce. Cover and refrigerate. For the filling, combine ground beef and seasonings in a separate bowl. Mix well. Shape into 4 patties. Grill, covered, over medium-to-high heat for 10 to 12 minutes or until meat is no longer pink, turning once. Cut patties into thin slices. Stuff into pitas. Add lettuce, tomato, and onion. Serve with yogurt sauce. Makes 4 servings.

# MAIN DISHES: PASTA

## BOW TIES WITH SAUSAGE, TOMATO, AND CREAM

*I cook one new recipe every week for my blog, so needless to say I have lots of recipes tucked away to make "someday soon." This recipe was in my file for years before I finally tried it, and boy, do I wish I'd given it a whirl sooner! This is an inexpensive dish that's absolutely delicious—plus you can plate it beautifully for company. Great stuff.*

1 (12-ounce) package bow tie pasta

1 tablespoon olive oil

1 pound sweet Italian turkey sausage (removed from the casing)

½ teaspoon red pepper flakes (decrease if your family doesn't like spicy dishes)

½ cup diced onion

3 cloves garlic, minced

1 (28-ounce) can Italian-style plum tomatoes, coarsely chopped

1½ cups heavy cream (or half-and-half to save on calories!)

½ teaspoon salt

3 tablespoons minced fresh parsley

Bring a large pot of lightly salted water to a boil. Cook pasta in boiling water for 8 to 10 minutes, until al dente; drain. Heat oil in a large, deep skillet over medium heat. Cook sausage until browned all over. Stir in onion and garlic, and cook until onion is tender.

Stir in tomatoes, cream, and salt. Simmer until mixture thickens, 8 to 10 minutes. Stir cooked pasta into sauce, and heat through. Sprinkle with parsley. Makes 4 to 6 servings.


## PRESTO PESTO PASTA CON POLLO

8 ounces bow tie pasta

8 ounces button mushrooms, sliced

2 tablespoons olive oil

1 (8.1-ounce) jar of pesto sauce

2 cups fresh baby spinach

2½ cups rotisserie chicken, diced

½ cup sun-dried tomatoes, cut into thin strips

1 lemon (zest and juice)

Salt and pepper to taste

Finely shredded Parmesan cheese (optional) for topping

In a 4-quart Dutch oven, cook pasta according to package directions. In a large sauté pan, cook mushrooms in olive oil (approximately 5 minutes) and season them to taste. Drain the cooked pasta, reserving ½ cup of the pasta water. In a small bowl, mix together the pesto and the ½ cup of pasta water to make a sauce. Sprinkle spinach on top of the mushrooms in the sauté pan and pour the hot pasta on top to help wilt the spinach. Add to the pasta mixture the rotisserie chicken, sun-dried tomatoes, zest and juice from a lemon, and pesto sauce. Give the mixture a gentle toss to combine. Season the pasta to taste. If desired, serve with a sprinkle of Parmesan cheese. Makes 4 servings.

# LINGUINE WITH WHITE CLAM SAUCE

1 pound linguine
1 tablespoon salt
¼ cup extra-virgin olive oil
2 tablespoons butter
4 cloves garlic, chopped
½ cup white wine
Juice and zest from 1 or 2 lemons
2 to 3 (15-ounce) cans whole baby clams, with their juice
Handful flat-leaf parsley, chopped

Bring a large pot of water to a boil. Add the linguine and salt and cook as directed or until al dente. The linguine will continue to cook in sauce, later. To a large skillet heated over medium heat, add oil, butter, and garlic. Cook together. Add the wine and the juice from the clams to the pan, then the zest of 1 or 2 lemons. Finally, add the clams. Drain pasta and add it to the clam sauce. Toss and coat the pasta in sauce with clams until the pasta absorbs the flavor and juices, 2 to 3 minutes. Remove from heat and season with salt, add parsley, and serve with a loaf of crusty bread. Makes 4 servings.

# HOMEMADE SPAGHETTI AND MEATBALLS

## Sauce

¾ cup chopped onion

5 cloves garlic, minced

¼ cup olive oil

2 (28-ounce) cans whole peeled tomatoes, undrained

2 teaspoons salt

1 teaspoon white sugar

1 (6-ounce) can tomato paste

¾ teaspoon dried basil

½ teaspoon black pepper

## Meatballs

*This recipe will make enough for a double batch, half to eat and half to freeze.*

½ cup plain bread crumbs

½ cup chopped fresh flat-leaf parsley

4 large eggs, lightly beaten

2 tablespoons whole milk

2 tablespoons ketchup

1½ cups grated Romano (or Parmesan) cheese

1½ teaspoons salt

1 teaspoon freshly ground black pepper

1 pound Italian turkey sausages, casings removed

1 pound ground beef

*To make sauce:* Sauté onion and garlic in ¼ cup olive oil until onion is translucent. Stir in tomatoes, salt, and sugar. Cover, reduce heat to medium-low, and simmer 1½ hours. Stir in tomato paste, basil, and ½ teaspoon pepper, and simmer 30 more minutes. Gently break apart the tomatoes with the back of your wooden spoon. Five to 10 minutes before serving, add in your meatballs and then serve over a big bowl of your favorite pasta.

*To make meatballs:* In a medium bowl, stir together the bread crumbs, parsley, eggs, milk, ketchup, Romano cheese, and the salt and pepper. Add the turkey and ground beef, then gently stir to combine. Make your meatballs the standard size and put them on a baking sheet. Bake at 400 degrees for 10 to 15 minutes. When done cooking, drop in the sauce for a few minutes. This will be just as delicious with a lot less mess. Makes 6 to 8 servings.

*Note*: Although you can buy bread crumbs at the store, making homemade bread crumbs for your dishes is easy and inexpensive. We had a loaf of French bread that wasn't being eaten, and I just cut the bread into chunks and gave it a whirl through the food processor. If your bread is not stale and needs a little more drying out, simply bake in a 300-degree oven for approximately 10 to 15 minutes; about halfway through, turn the bread over so it dries evenly. Remove from oven and let cool. Then put the bread in your food processor and pulse until you have your delicious bread crumbs.

I slip these into the freezer in freezer-safe containers until I need them for my recipes. Whenever your recipe calls for bread crumbs, just take a fork and gently scrape the bread crumbs to loosen them, measure, and add to any recipe. It is a great freezer staple that can be added to any time you have a little leftover bread (or even those ends of a bread loaf) on hand in the kitchen.

## MAIN DISHES: SEAFOOD

## PANKO-CRUSTED TILAPIA NUGGETS WITH FANCY DIPPING SAUCE

1½ pounds tilapia fillets, cut into wide strips

3 large eggs, lightly beaten

Coarse salt and pepper

2½ cups panko bread crumbs (in the international foods or baking aisle of your grocery store)

1 tablespoon and ¼ teaspoon Old Bay Seasoning, divided

2 tablespoons olive oil

½ cup light mayonnaise

¼ cup fresh parsley, chopped

1 tablespoon Dijon mustard

1 tablespoon fresh lemon juice, plus lemon wedges for serving

To make fish nuggets, cut tilapia fillets in half and then chunk into nugget-sized pieces. Preheat oven to 475 degrees, with racks in top and bottom third. Line 2 baking sheets with aluminum foil; set aside. Place egg in a wide shallow bowl; season with salt and pepper. In another bowl, combine panko, 1 tablespoon Old Bay, and oil. Dip tilapia into egg, shaking off excess, then into panko mixture, pressing to adhere. Place on prepared baking sheets. Bake until lightly browned, 12 to 15 minutes, rotating sheets from top to bottom halfway through.

Meanwhile, in a small bowl, stir together mayonnaise, parsley, mustard, lemon juice, and remaining Old Bay Seasoning. Season with salt and pepper. Serve fish sticks with dipping sauce. Makes 6 servings.

# MARINATED GRILLED SHRIMP

3 cloves garlic, minced
¼ cup olive oil
¼ cup tomato sauce
2 tablespoons red wine vinegar
2 tablespoons chopped fresh basil
½ teaspoon salt
¼ teaspoon cayenne pepper
1 pound fresh shrimp, peeled and deveined
Skewers

In a large bowl, stir together the garlic, olive oil, tomato sauce, and red wine vinegar. Season with basil, salt, and cayenne pepper. Add shrimp to the bowl, and stir until evenly coated. Cover and refrigerate for 1 to 2 hours, stirring once or twice. Preheat grill for medium heat. Thread shrimp onto skewers, piercing once near the tail and once near the head. Discard marinade. Lightly oil grill grate. Cook shrimp on preheated grill for 2 to 3 minutes per side, or until opaque. Makes 4 servings.

## HERB-BAKED TILAPIA

4 (4-to-6-ounce) tilapia fillets
⅓ cup Parmesan cheese
¼ cup low-fat mayonnaise
¼ cup dry bread crumbs (I prefer the Italian bread crumbs
     and I skip the dried seasonings)
1 teaspoon dried basil
1 teaspoon dried oregano
¼ teaspoon salt
¼ teaspoon pepper

Heat oven to 400 degrees. Place tilapia on a baking sheet. In a small bowl, combine cheese and mayonnaise. Spread evenly over fish. In another bowl, combine bread crumbs, basil, oregano, salt, and pepper. Sprinkle over fish. Coat fish lightly with cooking spray. Bake 10 minutes or until fish flakes easily with fork. Makes 4 servings.

## TILAPIA PITAS

½ cup mayonnaise
¼ cup Italian dressing
½ cup crumbled feta cheese
1 pinch cayenne pepper, or to taste
⅛ teaspoon ground black pepper, or to taste
1 pinch salt
3 tablespoons extra-virgin olive oil
1 pound tilapia fillets

Old Bay Seasoning (a generous sprinkle)
Salt and pepper to taste
6 pita breads, cut in half
2 cups romaine lettuce, chopped

In a small bowl, stir together the mayonnaise, Italian dressing, and feta cheese. Season with cayenne pepper (optional), black pepper, and salt. Mix until well blended, then set aside.

Heat oil in a large nonstick skillet over medium-high heat. Place the tilapia fillets in the skillet, and season with Old Bay Seasoning, salt, and pepper. Sauté until fish is browned on each side and flakes easily with a fork, 5 to 7 minutes. Warm pita breads in the toaster or in the microwave to soften. Open from the cut side to make pockets. Fill pita bread halves with tilapia fillets and lettuce, then spoon in some of the feta cheese sauce. Makes 4 servings.

## BALSAMIC AND ROSEMARY GRILLED SALMON

4 (4-ounce) salmon fillets
Sea salt to taste
1 tablespoon balsamic vinegar
3 tablespoons olive oil
¼ cup fresh-squeezed lemon juice
2 cloves garlic, minced
1 tablespoon fresh rosemary, minced

Season salmon fillets to taste with sea salt, and place into a shallow glass dish. Whisk together vinegar, olive oil, lemon juice, garlic, and rosemary; pour over salmon fillets. Cover and refrigerate for three hours. Preheat an outdoor grill for medium-high heat, and lightly oil grate. Remove salmon from marinade and shake off excess. Discard remaining marinade. Cook on preheated grill until fish is opaque in the center and flakes easily with a fork, about 4 minutes per side. Makes 4 servings.

## MAIN DISHES: PIZZA NIGHT

### BREAD MACHINE PIZZA DOUGH

1½ cups warm water

2 tablespoons and 1 teaspoon olive oil

4¼ cups bread flour

2 teaspoons salt

1 envelope (2¼ teaspoons) instant or rapid-rise yeast

To make this dough with the bread machine, add ingredients as follows: warm water, olive oil, flour, salt, and then yeast at the top. Turn machine on and select the dough setting. When the machine beeps, you can roll out the dough onto your pizza stone/pan.

*Note*: Because of the amount of dough this makes, I am able to make one large pizza and an order of cheese bread on the side. To make the cheese bread, just roll out the dough and then brush with olive oil and sprinkle garlic salt and Italian cheese blend or mozzarella cheese on top. I bake this at 450 degrees for 12 minutes or until the cheese and dough are a nice golden color. Serve with an extra side of sauce, highlighted in the pizza routine below.

## CLARK FAMILY FRIDAY-NIGHT PIZZA

1 can crushed tomatoes
1 teaspoon sugar
1 teaspoon salt
1 ball of pizza dough
1½ cups mozzarella cheese
½ cup 5- or 4-cheese blend
Toppings of your choice

Preheat oven to 450 degrees. While the oven is preheating, cook the crushed tomatoes, sugar, and salt in a pot over low heat for 15 minutes. Bake the crust only for 8 to 10 minutes. Pull the crust out and then top with the crushed tomatoes, mozzarella cheese, 5-cheese blend, and toppings of your choice. Put pizza back in and cook for 10 to 12 minutes or until the cheese is bubbly and the crust is nicely browned. Makes 4 servings.

## SAUCES

### FAST ENCHILADA SAUCE

1 tablespoon vegetable oil

1 onion, minced

½ teaspoon salt

3 tablespoons chili powder (this can be adjusted to your
   family's spice preference)

3 cloves garlic, minced

2 teaspoons cumin

2 teaspoons sugar

2 (8-ounce) cans tomato sauce

½ cup water

Salt and pepper to taste

Heat the oil in a 12-inch skillet over medium heat until simmering. Add the onion and salt and cook until onion softens, about 5 minutes. Stir in the chili powder, garlic, cumin, and sugar. Cook until fragrant, about 15 seconds. Stir in the tomato sauce and water. Bring to a simmer and cook until slightly thickened, about 5 minutes. Season with salt and pepper to taste. Makes approximately 3 cups.

## SWEET MUSTARD DIPPING SAUCE

½ cup Dijon mustard
¼ cup maple syrup
1 tablespoon brown sugar

Combine these 3 ingredients in a small bowl. Serve with your favorite pretzel or chicken tenders. Makes ¾ cup.

## HOMEMADE BARBECUE SAUCE

2 cups ketchup
4 tablespoons brown sugar
1 tablespoon Worcestershire sauce
1 tablespoon soy sauce
1 tablespoon vinegar
½ teaspoon garlic powder

Mix together all ingredients and serve with your choice of meat. Makes approximately 2 cups.

# SIDE DISHES: RICE, POTATOES, VEGETABLES, BREADS

## LEMON RICE PILAF

*This rice is a wonderful complement to my Lemon Chicken recipe and great with any kind of white fish.*

1 tablespoon extra-virgin olive oil
1 tablespoon butter
1 large shallot, finely chopped
1½ cups long-grain rice
½ cup dry white wine
3 sprigs of fresh thyme (approximately 1 tablespoon)
2 cups chicken broth or stock
1 cup water
1 lemon, zested
Fresh parsley

Heat a medium saucepan or pot over moderate heat. Add oil, butter, and shallot to the pan. Sauté shallot 2 minutes, then add the rice. Lightly brown rice 3 to 5 minutes. Add wine and allow it to evaporate entirely, 1 to 2 minutes. Add thyme and chicken broth to the rice. Add 1 cup water to pot. Bring liquid to a boil. Cover rice and reduce heat. Cook rice 20 minutes, until tender. Stir the lemon zest and parsley into rice. Transfer to dinner plates or warm serving dish. Makes 4 servings.

# RICE AND RONI

*Why pay for a sodium-ridden box of flavored rice when you can make your own homemade version? Throw in a little broccoli for even more color and a little added crunch.*

1 tablespoon oil
½ pound pasta, vermicelli, or spaghetti
1 cup long-grain rice
1 small onion, chopped
1 tablespoon chopped fresh parsley leaves, or 1 teaspoon
    dried parsley
2 cups chicken or beef broth

Begin by placing the oil in a pot and breaking the dried noodles into ½- to 1-inch pieces. Turn on medium-high heat and stir the noodles in the oil until they begin to brown slightly. Add the rice, onion, parsley, and broth. Stir mixture, cover tightly, and cook as you would regular rice, approximately 20 minutes. Fluff rice with a fork and serve. Makes 4 servings.

## MAKE-AHEAD MASHED POTATOES

5 pounds of potatoes
1 (8-ounce) package of low-fat cream cheese, softened
¾ cup low-fat sour cream
4 tablespoons butter, divided
¾ cup milk (or more if desired)
1½ teaspoons salt
Pinch of paprika

Peel potatoes and cut into small cubes. Put the potatoes in a large pot filled with cold water. Boil for 25 minutes or until fork-tender. Drain the potatoes and put them back into the hot pot. Add cream cheese, sour cream, 3 tablespoons of the butter, milk, and salt. Mash with a potato masher or use a hand mixer to whip the potatoes. Just before serving, brush the top of the potatoes with a tablespoon of butter and sprinkle with paprika. Makes enough to serve a crowd—at least 10 servings.

## CHEESY MASHED POTATOES

6 medium potatoes (peeled and cut into 1-inch cubes)
¾ cup evaporated milk
½ stick butter
1 cup shredded cheese (preferably cheddar)
Salt and pepper to taste

Place potatoes in large saucepan. Cover with water; bring to a boil. Cook over medium-high heat for 15 to 20 minutes or until tender; drain. Return potatoes to saucepan; add evaporated milk and butter. Beat with a handheld mixer until smooth. Stir in cheese. Season with salt and pepper. Makes 6 servings.

## SHOESTRING OVEN FRIES

4 russet potatoes, cut into thin wedges
3 tablespoons extra-virgin olive oil
1 teaspoon dried thyme
1 teaspoon dried oregano
Parmesan cheese

Preheat oven to 500 degrees. Slice potatoes into thin shoestrings and place them on a greased cookie sheet. Pour olive oil over the potatoes and then coat them with the seasonings. Using fingers, toss gently. Cook for 15 to 20 minutes or until the potatoes are done. Give them a generous shake of Parmesan cheese. Makes 6 to 8 servings.

## ROSEMARY AND CHEESE BREADSTICKS

1 cup grated Parmesan, Asiago, or Romano cheese
1 teaspoon chopped fresh rosemary leaves
1 package refrigerated breadsticks
1 tablespoon olive oil
Salt or garlic salt to taste

Preheat the oven to 350 degrees. Line two heavy baking sheets with silicone baking covers or parchment paper. Pour cheese and chopped fresh rosemary on a plate to roll the dough in. Separate the dough strips. Using a pizza cutter or a large sharp knife, cut each dough strip in half lengthwise to form thin strips. Working with one dough strip at a time, coat each strip with the cheese mixture, pressing very gently. Twist each cheese-covered strip and place onto prepared baking sheets. Drizzle with olive oil. Sprinkle with salt or garlic salt, to taste. Bake until the breadsticks are golden brown, about 10 to 15 minutes. Transfer the warm breadsticks to a basket or tall glass and serve. Makes 4 servings.

## SWEET CORNBREAD

1 cup all-purpose flour

1 cup yellow cornmeal

⅔ cup white sugar

1 teaspoon salt

3 teaspoons baking powder

1 egg

1 cup milk

⅓ cup vegetable oil

Preheat oven to 400 degrees. Spray or lightly grease a 9-inch round cake pan. In a large bowl, combine flour, cornmeal, sugar, salt, and baking powder. Stir in egg, milk, and vegetable oil until well combined. Pour batter into prepared pan. Bake for 20 to 25 minutes. Makes 6 servings.

# PUMPKIN CORNBREAD MUFFINS

*I don't want to toot my own horn, but these Pumpkin Cornbread Muffins may have made me famous in some small circles. You won't believe what a delicious flavor combination this is, and the raw sugar sprinkled on top adds a hint of crunch to these decadent muffins.*

1¼ cups flour
¾ cup cornmeal
⅔ cup light brown sugar
1 tablespoon baking powder
½ teaspoon salt
½ teaspoon nutmeg
½ teaspoon cinnamon
¾ cup canned pumpkin puree
¾ cup buttermilk (I substitute with regular milk and a
    teaspoon of vinegar to sour)
¼ cup butter, melted
2 eggs, at room temperature
2 tablespoons honey
Sugar for sprinkling (I prefer raw sugar)

Preheat oven to 350 degrees. Line a muffin tin with paper or foil liners. In a bowl, mix together flour, cornmeal, sugar, baking powder, salt, nutmeg, and cinnamon. In another mixing bowl, mix with a wooden spoon the pumpkin puree, buttermilk, butter, eggs, and honey, until well combined. Add the pumpkin mixture to the flour mixture just until combined. Transfer to the prepared tin. Sprinkle a little sugar (I use raw sugar) on top. Bake for about 20 to 25 minutes, or until edges just begin to color. Cool to room temperature. Makes approximately 12 muffins.

# ROASTED GREEN BEANS

*These roasted green beans are the only kind of green beans my children will eat. I have a hard time getting these on the table and not nibbling away at the tray of them before we eat. I guarantee that this is a foolproof way to get your kids to eat their vegetables*

2 pounds fresh green beans (or a bag of frozen fancy green beans)
Salt and pepper to taste
Zest from one or two lemons, juice reserved
2 tablespoons minced garlic (I use bottled garlic to save a little time)
1 to 2 tablespoons olive oil

Preheat oven to 400 degrees. Put green beans on a jelly roll pan. Sprinkle salt and pepper, lemon zest, and garlic over the beans. Drizzle the olive oil over the green beans and then toss with your hands until they are all coated with seasonings and zest. Spread out in a single layer on a cookie sheet and put into the oven. Roast fresh green beans for 20 to 25 minutes and roast frozen green beans for an additional 10 minutes. When they are done, pull from the oven and put them on a serving platter. Squeeze the reserved lemon juice over the top and serve. Makes 6 to 8 servings.

## SIMPLE ROASTED ASPARAGUS

1 bunch thin asparagus spears, trimmed
2 tablespoons olive oil
1 clove garlic, minced (optional)
1 teaspoon sea salt
½ teaspoon ground black pepper
Parmesan cheese (optional)

Preheat oven to 425 degrees. Arrange the asparagus in a single layer on a cookie sheet and drizzle with olive oil. Toss to coat the spears, then sprinkle with garlic, salt, and pepper. Rub the flavors into your asparagus with clean hands. Bake in the preheated oven until just tender, 12 to 15 minutes depending on thickness. After you pull the asparagus out of the oven, dust with a little Parmesan cheese. Makes 4 servings.

## HONEY-GLAZED CARROTS

2 tablespoons butter
4 tablespoons honey
1 pound peeled baby carrots
Salt and pepper to taste

In a small saucepan, melt butter. Add honey, stirring until completely incorporated. Remove from heat and set aside. Steam carrots just until they are bright orange (approximately 2 minutes) or to desired doneness. Place carrots in serving bowl and drizzle with honey glaze. Toss the carrots until they are thoroughly coated.

Season with salt and pepper to taste. Serve hot. Makes 6 to 8 servings.

## BREAKFAST

## BAKED SNICKERDOODLE DOUGHNUTS

*My husband's favorite cookie in the world is the snickerdoodle. I couldn't wait to create a batch of these doughnuts for him that would mimic his favorite flavors. I just know you will love them, too.*

2 cups cake flour (or 1¾ cups all-purpose flour plus ¼ cup cornstarch)
¾ cup sugar
1 teaspoon cinnamon
2 teaspoons baking powder
1 teaspoon salt
¾ cup milk
2 eggs, lightly beaten
2 tablespoons butter
1 teaspoon vanilla extract

### Cinnamon and Sugar Topping
¼ cup butter, melted
⅓ cup sugar
1 teaspoon cinnamon powder

Preheat oven to 400 degrees. Whisk together the cake flour, sugar, cinnamon, baking powder, and salt in a large bowl. Pour in the milk, eggs, butter, and vanilla extract. Gently mix the ingredients together. Be careful not to overmix the batter. Lightly grease a doughnut pan with nonstick cooking spray. Carefully spoon the batter into the doughnut pan, filling each one halfway (you should get 12 doughnuts total). Bake the doughnuts at 400 degrees for 8 minutes. The doughnuts will remain light in color, but should spring back when pressed. Allow to cool for 5 minutes. Unmold each doughnut gently and lightly brush each with reserved ¼ cup melted butter. Dunk in a bowl with the sugar and cinnamon. Shake off excess sugar and serve immediately. Makes 1 dozen doughnuts.

## BAKED BLUEBERRY DOUGHNUTS WITH LEMON GLAZE

### Doughnuts

    2 cups cake flour (or 1¾ cup all-purpose flour plus ¼ cup
        cornstarch)
    ¾ cup sugar
    2 teaspoons baking powder
    1 teaspoon salt
    Zest from 1 lemon
    ¾ cup milk
    2 eggs, lightly beaten
    2 tablespoons butter
    1 teaspoon vanilla extract
    ½ cup blueberries, halved

### Lemon Glaze

    1½ cups powdered sugar
    1 tablespoon milk
    1 tablespoon lemon juice (from the lemon you zested)
    ½ teaspoon vanilla extract

Preheat oven to 400 degrees. Whisk together the cake flour, sugar, baking powder, and salt in a large bowl. Add the lemon zest and whisk. Pour in the milk, eggs, butter, and vanilla extract. Gently mix the ingredients together, being careful not to overmix the batter. Gently fold in the halved blueberries. Lightly grease a doughnut pan with nonstick cooking spray. Carefully spoon the batter into the doughnut pan, filling each one halfway. Bake the doughnuts for 8 to 9 minutes. The doughnuts will remain light in color, but should spring back when pressed.

*For the glaze:* Put the powdered sugar in a large bowl. Add the milk, lemon juice, and vanilla extract. Whisk to combine. If the glaze is too thick, add additional lemon juice or milk, ½ teaspoon at a time until desired consistency is reached. Once the doughnuts are done baking, let them cool in the doughnut pan for 4 minutes. Carefully remove the doughnuts from the pan. Dip one side of each doughnut in the glaze. Set the doughnuts on top of a cooling rack with a baking sheet underneath. Allow the glaze on the doughnuts to dry and serve immediately with big glasses of ice-cold milk. Makes 1 dozen doughnuts.

# WHOLE-WHEAT CINNAMON WAFFLES

*I love these waffles because they've got a little extra nutritional value from the wheat flour and wheat germ—but my kids would never dream they were anything but a treat. I have found that the best flour for these is the whole-wheat white flour because it produces a light and fluffy-textured waffle while still providing whole grains to their diet.*

1¾ cups whole-wheat white flour

¼ cup wheat germ

⅓ cup instant nonfat dry milk powder

1 tablespoon ground cinnamon

1 tablespoon baking powder

½ teaspoon baking soda

½ teaspoon salt

2 eggs

3 tablespoons canola oil

2 cups buttermilk (or use regular milk and add
    2 tablespoons of vinegar and let stand for
    5 minutes)

2 teaspoons vanilla extract

In a large bowl, combine the flour, wheat germ, dry milk, cinnamon, baking powder, baking soda, and salt; mix well. In a medium bowl, mix the eggs, oil, buttermilk, and vanilla. Pour over the dry ingredients. Do not overmix. Coat your waffle iron with vegetable cooking spray and preheat. Pour ½ cup of the batter into the center of the hot waffle iron and cook until the batter stops steaming, about 6 minutes. Cooking time varies according to the type of waffle iron you have, but you'll quickly get a feel for how long yours takes. Repeat with remainder of the dough, applying the cooking spray between waffles. Serve warm with your favorite syrup. Makes 4 servings.

## OATMEAL COOKIE WAFFLES

*This is one of my oldest and most favorite waffle recipes. They are deeply satisfying and are created using budget-friendly pantry ingredients.*

4 cups quick oats (grind the oats in your food processor or
    blender until it is a fine powder)
1 cup all-purpose flour
2 teaspoons salt
3 cups milk (you can use prepared powdered milk)
2 tablespoons baking powder
2 eggs, beaten
2 tablespoons molasses
4 tablespoons canola oil
2 teaspoons vanilla
2 teaspoons cinnamon
¼ cup sugar

Mix all ingredients together until there are no lumps. Pour batter into well-greased waffle iron and allow each waffle to cook until it stops steaming—usually 4 to 6 minutes, depending on your waffle maker. Serve immediately. Makes 4 servings.

# LIGHT AND FLUFFY PUMPKIN PANCAKES

1¼ cups all-purpose flour

2 tablespoons sugar

2 teaspoons baking powder

½ teaspoon cinnamon

½ teaspoon ginger

½ teaspoon nutmeg

1 pinch clove

½ teaspoon salt

1¼ cups low-fat milk

⅓ cup canned pumpkin puree

2 tablespoons melted butter

1 egg

Whisk flour, sugar, baking powder, spices, and salt in a bowl. In a separate bowl, whisk together milk, pumpkin, melted butter, and egg. Fold mixture into dry ingredients. Spray or grease a skillet and heat over medium heat; pour in ¼ cup batter for each pancake. Cook pancakes about 3 minutes per side. This recipe makes 6 6-inch pancakes.

*Note*: This can easily be doubled and frozen or stored in the refrigerator for a great breakfast later in the week.

## OVERNIGHT SAUSAGE BREAKFAST CASSEROLE (SLOW COOKER)

*This is a slow cooker favorite of our family, particularly for Sunday brunch. I can set the slow cooker in the morning, and we can come home after church and eat right away. You can make cleanup a little easier by spraying your slow cooker with nonstick spray before putting in the ingredients.*

1 pound turkey sausage (sweet or spicy)
1 teaspoon mustard powder
½ teaspoon salt
4 eggs, beaten
2 cups milk
6 slices white bread, toasted and cut into cubes
8 ounces shredded cheddar cheese

Crumble sausage and cook thoroughly. Drain fat. In a large bowl, mix all ingredients together evenly. Place the casserole in the fridge overnight. In the morning, put in the slow cooker for 4 hours on high or 6 hours on low. Serve with a side of fresh fruit and juice. Makes 4 to 6 servings.

## HOMEMADE PANCAKE SYRUP

3 cups granulated sugar
1½ cups water
3 tablespoons molasses
1 teaspoon vanilla
2 teaspoons butter flavoring
1 teaspoon maple extract

In a large pot, bring all of the ingredients to a boil, stirring until the sugar dissolves. Turn off burner, but leave pot on burner until the bubbling stops. Makes 2 cups syrup.

## SNACKS AND DESSERTS

### HOMEMADE CHOCOLATE SYRUP

½ cup cocoa
1 cup water
2 cups sugar
⅛ teaspoon salt
¼ teaspoon vanilla

Mix the cocoa and the water in a saucepan. Heat and stir to dissolve the cocoa. Add the sugar and stir to dissolve. Boil 3 minutes. Add the salt and vanilla. Pour into a sterilized pint jar, and store covered in the refrigerator. Makes 1 cup syrup.

## HOMEMADE SWEETENED CONDENSED MILK

1 cup instant nonfat dry milk solids
⅔ cup sugar
⅓ cup boiling water
3 tablespoons melted margarine

Combine all ingredients and process with an electric mixer until smooth. This can be stored in the refrigerator until it is ready to be used. Makes equivalent of 1 can sweetened condensed milk.

## DELICIOUSLY HOMEMADE GRANOLA BARS

2 cups rolled oats
¾ cup packed brown sugar
½ cup wheat germ
1 teaspoon ground cinnamon
1 cup all-purpose flour
¾ cup mini chocolate chips
1 teaspoon salt
½ cup honey
1 egg, beaten
½ cup canola oil
2 teaspoons vanilla extract

Preheat the oven to 350 degrees. Generously grease a 9-by-13-inch baking pan. In a large bowl, mix together the oats, brown sugar, wheat germ, cinnamon, flour, mini chocolate chips, and salt. Make a well in the center, and pour in the honey, egg, oil, and vanilla. Mix well using a wooden spoon. Pat the mixture evenly into the prepared pan. Bake for 30 minutes in the preheated oven, until the bars begin to turn golden at the edges. Cool for 5 minutes, then cut into bars while still warm. Makes approximately 10 servings.

## CHOCOLATE CHIP COOKIE BARS

2¼ cups all-purpose flour

1 teaspoon baking soda

1 teaspoon salt

1 cup butter, softened

¾ cup granulated sugar

¾ cup packed brown sugar

1 teaspoon vanilla extract

2 eggs

1 (12-ounce) package semisweet chocolate chips

1 cup chopped nuts (optional)

Preheat oven to 375 degrees. Grease a 9-by-13-inch pan. Combine flour, baking soda, and salt in a small bowl. Beat butter, both sugars, and vanilla in large mixing bowl. Add eggs 1 at a time, beating well after each. Gradually beat flour mixture into butter mixture. Stir in chocolate chips and nuts. Spread into prepared pan. Bake 30 to 35 minutes or until golden brown. Makes approximately 12 servings.

*Note:* I recommend using a plastic knife to cut these out to get a perfectly cut bar with minimal crumbs.

## BANANA CRUMB MUFFINS

*These muffins look like something you would purchase from a bakery with their beautiful streusel topping. I wrap these individually and keep them in a basket by our door to be munched on throughout the day. These are one of our favorite treats!*

1½ cups all-purpose flour
1 teaspoon baking soda
1 teaspoon baking powder
½ teaspoon salt
3 bananas, mashed
¾ cup white sugar
1 egg, lightly beaten
⅓ cup butter, melted
½ cup packed brown sugar
⅛ cup all-purpose flour
½ teaspoon ground cinnamon
1 tablespoon butter

Preheat oven to 375 degrees. Lightly grease ten muffin cups or line with muffin papers. In a large bowl, mix together flour, baking soda, baking powder, and salt. In another bowl, beat together bananas, sugar, egg, and melted butter. Stir the banana mixture into the flour mixture just until moistened. Spoon batter into prepared muffin cups. In a small bowl, mix together brown sugar, flour, and cinnamon. Cut in the butter until mixture resembles coarse cornmeal. Sprinkle topping over muffins. Bake in preheated oven for 18 to 20 minutes, or until a toothpick inserted into center of muffins comes out clean. Makes 1 dozen muffins.

## EASY BROWNIES

*These brownies are like a little piece of heaven and super easy to make. If you are a brownie-mix kind of mom, I guarantee that these are just as simple as the mix and are great to try when making your first batch of the homemade variety.*

2 ounces unsweetened chocolate
1 stick butter
1 cup sugar
2 eggs
½ cup flour
½ cup semisweet chocolate chips

Preheat oven to 375 degrees. In microwave, melt chocolate and butter for 1 minute. Stir and then heat again until melted; allow mixture to cool. In a bowl, beat sugar and eggs. Stir in the cooled chocolate, flour, and chips. Pour mixture into an 8-by-8-inch pan (not greased). Bake for 15 to 20 minutes. Mixture will appear a little gooey due to the chocolate chips so be careful not to over-cook. Makes approximately 8 servings.

## EASY CAKE-MIX PEANUT BUTTER COOKIES

1 (18.25-ounce) package yellow cake mix
1 cup creamy peanut butter
½ cup vegetable oil
2 eggs
2 tablespoons water

Preheat oven to 350 degrees. Pour the cake mix into a large bowl. Make a well in the center, and add peanut butter, oil, eggs, and water. Mix until well blended. Drop by teaspoonfuls onto ungreased cookie sheets. Flatten slightly using a fork dipped in water. Bake for 10 to 12 minutes in the preheated oven. Let cookies set on cookie sheet for 2 to 3 minutes before carefully removing from the cookie sheet to cool on wire racks. Makes 2 dozen cookies.

## HEAVENLY BANANA BREAD

2 cups all-purpose flour

1 teaspoon baking soda

¼ teaspoon salt

½ cup butter

¾ cup brown sugar

2 eggs beaten

2⅓ cups mashed overripe bananas (about 4 bananas)

1 teaspoon vanilla

½ teaspoon cinnamon

Preheat oven to 350. Grease a loaf pan with a small amount of butter or cooking spray. Dust with flour. In a large bowl, combine flour, baking soda, and salt. In a separate bowl, cream together butter and brown sugar. Stir in eggs and mashed bananas until well blended. Add vanilla and cinnamon. Stir banana mixture into flour mixture; mix just to moisten. Pour batter into prepared loaf pan. Bake 60 to 65 minutes. Allow bread to cool 10 minutes in pan and then turn onto wire rack. Makes 1 loaf.

# CHOCOLATE BUTTERSCOTCH COOKIES

4½ cups all-purpose flour

2 teaspoons baking soda

2 cups butter, softened

1½ cups packed brown sugar

½ cup white sugar

2 (3.4-ounce) packages instant chocolate pudding mix

4 eggs

2 teaspoons vanilla extract

4 cups butterscotch chips

Preheat oven to 350 degrees. Sift together the flour and baking soda and set aside. In a large bowl, cream together the butter, brown sugar, and white sugar. Beat in the instant pudding and mix until blended. Stir in the eggs and vanilla. Blend in flour mixture. Finally, stir in butterscotch chips. Drop dough by spoonfuls on an ungreased cookie sheet. Bake 10 to 12 minutes. Edges should be golden brown. Makes 2 to 3 dozen cookies.

# RAINBOW CAKE IN A JAR WITH CLOUD FROSTING

*Individual rainbow cakes are a festive way to celebrate St. Patrick's Day. These cupcakes in half-pint jars are topped with a light frosting for a surprisingly light and fun snack. These are quite a project to make, but they are so fun and unusual, they make a perfect mommy-and-me project for a rainy day.*

## Cakes

½ stick unsalted butter

1½ cups sugar

2 eggs

2 teaspoons pure vanilla extract

2½ teaspoons baking powder

¼ teaspoon salt

2½ cups flour

1¼ cups milk

Betty Crocker Neon Gel Food Colors or Wilton food
    coloring (for bright rainbow colors)

8 to 10 half-pint jars

Cooking spray

Sprinkles

## Frosting

¾ cup sugar

¼ teaspoon cream of tartar

1 teaspoon vanilla extract

3 unbeaten egg whites

¼ cup boiling water

Preheat oven to 375 degrees. Take off the screw caps on the jars. Spray with nonstick cooking spray. Set aside. Put butter in mixer and beat at medium speed until somewhat smooth. Pour in sugar and beat well. Add 2 eggs. Mix well. Add vanilla, baking powder, salt, flour, and milk. Beat until well mixed. Divide your batter into 6 separate bowls (approximately 2 large ice cream scoops of batter into each bowl for even distribution). Tint your batter the colors of the rainbow—red, orange, yellow, green, blue, and violet. Using a small spoon, carefully spoon in each color of batter into layers or use a Ziploc bag and cut the tip off one corner of the bag to pipe each layer into the jars. Place jars in a 9-by-13-inch baking pan (with rim) and fill with ½ cup of water to create a water bath for your cake. Bake for 25 to 40 minutes or until your cake springs back and a skewer poked in the center comes out clean (length of time will depend entirely on how tall you stacked your batter!). While the cakes are cooling, make your frosting. Mix sugar, cream of tartar, vanilla, and egg whites. Add boiling water. Beat on high setting until the mixture forms peaks (about 7 minutes). Spoon frosting on cakes and finish with rainbow sprinkles. Makes 8 cakes.

## PARTY PUNCH

2 liters strawberry-flavored soda

2 liters 7Up Cherry

1 (12-ounce) can frozen pink lemonade concentrate

1 can pineapple juice

Mix all the ingredients together for the punch. This will fill 1 large punch bowl or 2 smaller ones.

## PARTY PUNCH ICE RING

Orange slices
Lemon slices
Lime slices
1 (8-ounce) jar Maraschino cherries
Cherry juice or red food coloring
Water
Metal ring mold (I use my Bundt pan for this one)

Create your ice ring by putting the citrus fruit slices in the ring mold, then pouring in the jar of cherries (juice and all). Top the Bundt pan off with water and freeze overnight. To serve, unmold ice ring into punch bowl and then add your party punch ingredients.

## HOMEMADE PUMPKIN SPICE LATTE

2 cups milk
1 cup very strong coffee (4 tablespoons coffee grounds to
    1 cup of hot water, if prepared in a French press)
2 tablespoons vanilla
4 teaspoons sugar
½ teaspoon pumpkin pie spice or cinnamon spice
2 heaping spoonfuls of pumpkin

Pour all of the ingredients into a pot and heat over medium-high heat until the coffee is steaming hot, whisking with a wire whisk until the ingredients are incorporated and a little frothy. Pour into mugs and top with fresh whipped cream and cinnamon. Enjoy!

*Notes:* If you are not a fan of the cinnamon texture, adding a cinnamon stick to the coffee mixture while heating it can be a great remedy. This way you get all of the cinnamon taste, but none of the grit.

This is just a base recipe that can be played with to your own tastes and preferences. It is meant to be personalized depending on how you like your latte.

If you like this recipe, be sure to visit MomAdvice.com for a half-dozen other great Starbucks knockoff drinks!

## AMY'S VERSION OF STARBUCKS' ICED PEPPERMINT MOCHA

*Don't throw away that last half cup of coffee! If you keep an ice-cube tray in your freezer for leftover coffee, you'll always have the main ingredient on hand to make yourself a fancy iced mocha. Look out, Starbucks!*

6 to 7 coffee ice cubes

4 tablespoons sugar (or to taste)

A generous squirt of chocolate syrup (approximately ⅛ cup)

1 tablespoon peppermint syrup (purchased behind the counter at Starbucks)

1 cup prepared powdered milk or regular milk

Place all ingredients into the blender and blend until smooth. This will yield 1 huge mocha or 2 smaller mochas.

## HOMEMADE COCOA MIX

*We go through two or three batches of this cocoa each winter in our house. Last year, I let my children paint their own cocoa mugs, which makes them love this treat all the more (we bought bargain-store mugs and used an easy porcelain paint set from Michaels—bought with a coupon of course). In the fall, when the kids help their dad rake leaves, I bring them cocoa to drink outside when they take a break—and I'd have to say they seem to love their favorite drink even more on the front porch than they do in the kitchen.*

4 cups nonfat dry milk powder
1½ cups sugar
1 cup nondairy coffee creamer
⅔ cup unsweetened cocoa powder
1 (4-ounce) package instant chocolate pudding mix

Place all ingredients in a large bowl and mix together. Place mix in a sifter and sift to make a really fine powder (or you can use your food processor for this step). Store in an airtight container. Add ½ cup of mix to an 8-ounce mug and fill with hot water.

## HOMEMADE CHAI TEA MIX

*You know, every once in a while you get so tied up with a recipe that people come looking for it when they visit you. That's how things are for me and this tea. I make a batch each fall and love to sip it on chilly afternoons. The funny thing is, though, that since I've been making it, my friends and neighbors love to sip it on chilly afternoons, too. People who know me come to my house expecting a homemade cup of this good stuff. Since it's such a hit for my friends and family, I also sometimes make batches of the mix in decorated jars to give as gifts.*

1 cup nonfat dry milk powder

1 cup powdered nondairy creamer

1 cup French vanilla powdered nondairy creamer

2½ cups white sugar

1½ cups unsweetened instant tea

2 teaspoons ground ginger

2 teaspoons ground cinnamon

1 teaspoon ground cloves

1 teaspoon ground cardamom

1 teaspoon nutmeg

1 teaspoon allspice

¼ teaspoon white pepper

Combine all ingredients in a food processor and blend until it is a fine powder. Add 2 to 3 tablespoons of mix to 8 ounces of hot water or milk.

## HOMEMADE MINT TRUFFLE CREAMER (WITH VARIATIONS)

1 can sweetened condensed milk

1½ cups nonfat milk (or you can use prepared powdered milk)

3 tablespoons unsweetened cocoa

3 tablespoons peppermint coffee syrup (or more depending on your personal taste)

Blend all ingredients together in your blender. Pour into a mason jar or your old coffee creamer dispenser. This creamer will keep up to 2 weeks in the fridge.

## Variations

To make French Vanilla Creamer, omit cocoa and peppermint syrup and add 1 tablespoon vanilla.

To make Chocolate Almond Creamer, omit peppermint syrup and add 1 teaspoon almond extract.

To make Amaretto Creamer, omit cocoa and peppermint and add ½ teaspoon cinnamon and 1 teaspoon almond extract.

# 4

...............

# Good Times: Holidays, Family Gatherings, and Special Occasions

I f there's one thing that sets our home apart, I hope it's our family's strong sense of tradition and closeness—especially when holidays, family gatherings, and special occasions roll around. This is something that's always been important to me, and it has become even more so since I've become a mom. As a frugal homemaker, I've found that special occasions are a time when being creative and choosing to open my heart instead of my wallet makes it possible to work wonders with a limited budget. Our family focuses on the joy of each event together, on traditions that make the people we love feel special, and on activities that remind us how fortunate we are.

Think about the very best holidays and special occasions in your life. I bet the things that make most of them wonderful aren't the presents or expensive trappings, but the feelings of warmth, happiness, and closeness to family and friends. Some of my own fondest memories are of things like snuggling up to read Christmas books with my children, watching them giggle with their dad while they drink cocoa on a crisp fall day, and creating a romantic Valentine's day at home with my husband. Every holiday, birthday, and anniversary we celebrate is about something other than money and presents, and choosing to focus on that has been a huge blessing for all of us.

Make it your goal to leave your family with a legacy of happy memories, not expensive gifts, and you'll be well on your way to creating the kinds of special times they'll always hold in their hearts.

## The Frugal First Step

There are so many wonderful, creative ways to make good times special for your family, but first things first: Let's talk about the budget. For every joyful way a mom can think of to celebrate a holiday, a birthday, or a special occasion, there's a way for it to bust her budget. Everything from decorating to special dinners to dress-up clothes, party favors, gifts, and travel expenses are extras, falling outside your family's day-to-day budget and potentially wreaking havoc with it. Any one of these costs is enough to derail a tight budget—as a group, they can constitute a financial crisis.

Of course, nobody wants to be a scrooge, bah-humbugging special-occasion expenses left and right. So what's a mom to do? My philosophy is simple: First, set a modest budget and stick to it. Second, think small, thoughtful, and memorable, and you'll find you can create wonderful special occasions without spending yourself into trouble.

## ESTIMATE YOUR EXPENSES

The first thing you need to do is get a handle on what exactly your special occasions are going to cost. I get so many emails from moms who suddenly find themselves looking at hundreds or even thousands of extra dollars in bills after a holiday is over, and they're not even sure where they spent it! Don't let this happen to you. *Before* you hit the mall or the market, figure out what you're going to buy and what you're going to skip. Think of it just like making your weekly or biweekly grocery list. Write down your anticipated spending on decorations, gifts, food, travel, and entertainment, and if you have to go over, know exactly where and why, so you can make it up ASAP. How much you budget for each occasion is a personal decision, but in our family, I try to keep spending for family birthdays under one hundred dollars, holiday meals with guests under fifty dollars, and Christmas spending at between four and five hundred dollars for all of our family gifts. We spend about one hundred on each child (which includes special gifts from the North Pole) and one hundred dollars total on each other. During the years when we have been most frugal, my hubby and I agreed to skip exchanging gifts with each other to keep costs down. The other two hundred dollars is spent on gifts for immediate family members, friends, teachers, and hostess gifts. I always keep them small, but these little gifts add up, so I always figure them in my budget.

## FIND THE FUNDS

We all know even the most modest holiday budget can seem out of range for a family struggling to make ends meet. With a little planning and clearly defined limits, though, it is possible to make an affordable, special holiday or occasion for your family.

**Hide away your holiday dollars.** One of my favorite ways to organize my budget is by setting up separate accounts for things that are important to us. I never use credit cards—if I want something badly enough, I figure out a way to save for it. And I do really want nice holidays for my family. My husband and I have a Christmas club account to save for holiday expenses. You've probably heard of these—a lot of our mothers and grandmothers faithfully put a few dollars a week in them decades ago to save for the holidays. Sometime after the 1970s, Christmas club accounts lost some of their popularity (might I guess because of the rise of easy credit cards?), but many banks and credit unions still offer this simple way to save. I love knowing that I am paying ahead my family's holiday—and that I won't put us in debt when the holiday season arrives.

My husband and I have an automatic withdrawal from our primary bank account that puts a small deposit—ten or twenty dollars a week, depending on how times are—into a Christmas account all year long. When we withdraw it in November or December, we have our holiday budget, free and clear of the guilt, interest, and potential woes of overspending on a credit card.

**Layaway.** Another way to make purchases without going into debt is with store layaway programs. This is a great choice in the event of a sale where you want to be sure you get the best price on particular items. Most stores don't offer layaway on Black Friday, but other sales are usually fair game. Walmart and Kmart, along with many other retailers, offer layaway programs. A five-dollar fee is the norm, but be sure you read the fine print so you know their program is one that works for you. I know people who do all their holiday shopping on one day in early fall, put it all on layaway, and then just focus on paying it off in time for Christmas. No matter how you use this program, it helps you stay out of debt and still buy the gifts you want at the best price available.

## GET THE MOST FOR YOUR MONEY

I'm a firm believer that no matter what you're buying, if you put your mind to it, you can find a way to buy it more economically. When it comes to buying gifts and holiday wares, planning ahead is the single biggest key to savings. Try these tips to make the most of your special-occasion budget:

**Shop off-season.** I know you've heard this one before, but I can't stress enough that a mom who doesn't mind thinking ahead and finding a little storage space can save an absolute fortune by shopping after-Christmas, end-of-summer, and other off-season sales. I hate to shop—but going shopping a week after Christmas or the last week of August and picking up super bargains for next year's gifts is worth the aggravation every time. Buy your daughter's Easter dress in May for the next year and you'll get half or more off; Halloween costumes get marked down by as much as 75 percent the day after the holiday; and summer-season decorations, party favors, plus all those gift-ready picnic supplies are always sold at cut-rate prices by the end of summer.

**Buy in bulk.** To keep spending down on gifts, I love to think of gifts that I can give in bulk to cut down on the expense of supplies and materials. Think of a craft, food gift, or gift basket that you could create that would fit many recipients. If you have a good friend that has the same gift in mind, you could also consider splitting the cost and assembling your gifts together.

By creating a gift in bulk, you can cut down on the expense of each individual gift.

I've made ribbon bookmarks and hair accessories to give in a small basket, and one of my favorite holiday gift ideas was gift boxes with my homemade hot chocolate mix, vanilla chai tea mix, and my peppermint candy cane bath salt mix. A friend and I got together and shared the cost of all the materials for these gifts, then spent an afternoon putting together all the mixes and assembling the baskets. At the end of a few hours of girl talk, we had enough of these lovely gift sets to give to lots of our friends, neighbors, and favorite teachers.

**Sign up for daily deal sites.** Daily deal sites can be a great way to snag holiday gifts for a fraction of the price. Sites like LivingSocial.com, DealRadar.com, and Groupon.com offer a daily deal to your favorite local shops for up to half the price that you would pay retail. Use these vouchers to buy your gifts for a lot less. You'll get a great gift to give and your recipient will never know what a bargain you got.

## SET REALISTIC EXPECTATIONS

If your children are young, do yourself a huge favor and start right now making sure the things they appreciate about holidays and special days are the experiences they enjoy, not the goods they get. So many children are raised to be waiting for the next big gift or an abundance of presents for their birthdays, for Christmas— heck, even for Valentine's Day, Easter, and the first day of school. Think of Dudley, the spoiled cousin in the Harry Potter series, counting his birthday gifts and having a fit because there are "only thirteen." Yikes!

In addition to keeping your family's focus away from sheer

materialism, choose your own boundaries and limits when exchanging gifts with the other special folks in your life as well:

**Think age appropriate and long term.** I know an eight-year-old who owns not only nearly every toy designed for a kid his age or younger, but also a phone, a camera, an iPod, an iPad, and a laptop. I'm sure you know one, too. The question I always ask myself (but try not to ask anyone else out loud) is, simply: What are these parents thinking? I was brought up to believe that if a person really wants something, she'd better wait and save and hope and pray . . . you know what I mean. How can a child possibly fully appreciate the joys of that first camera, first phone, first computer—when he or she has already got it all before the third grade?

I know some parents worry that their kid will be the last one, or the only one, who doesn't have something his or her peers are already enjoying. To be honest, sometimes I worry about this, too. But my experience has overwhelmingly been that once you make up your mind to pace your child's steps into the world of expensive technology and costly gifts, you will find you are definitely not alone. There are so many other parents struggling with the same choices—for a lot of different, good reasons. As you stand firm and choose age-appropriate gifts for your children, you will inevitably discover that your child is in very good company in having to wait for big-ticket items.

Make gift giving predictable for your children, so they have some idea what they might and might not expect. For example, some families give three gifts at Christmas, symbolizing the gift of the three kings. In our family, we follow a holiday gift tradition I read about years ago and give four gifts that represent something we want, something we need, something to wear, and something to read. At birthdays, keep gift giving simple—a special gift or two to mark the occasion—not to overwhelm it.

**Choose your customs—don't let them choose you.** If you have family or friends you shop for, take a minute to consider whether you enjoy and want to do this or not. If the answer is no, for whatever reason, have a frank conversation with your siblings, neighbors, or coworkers and simply suggest that since you're all adults and really pressed for time and money, why don't you all get together for a drink or an appetizer party or something equally fun and cost-effective, and phase out the gift giving ASAP.

**Set price limits, and stick to them.** In our extended family, we draw names in November and only exchange gifts with one person each. Like every gift exchange, this one has to have rules—and one of those rules is about how much the gift can cost. If you only want a twenty-dollar gift exchange and not the fifty-dollar one your sister-in-law or brother is pushing for, stick to your guns. I never feel embarrassed about taking a stand to keep these limits low. I also go to a lot of trouble to choose a thoughtful gift for my recipients. After all, there's really not much satisfaction in buying, or receiving, a gift card. I try to always give a gift.

My best friend and I have raised the gift price limit to an art form. Every year, we set a date when we will have dinner together (eating out is a very rare occasion for me, so this alone is special). We go out on a bargain-meal night, and then exchange our twenty-dollar gifts. Over the years, we've come to consider the limit a challenge, each trying to outdo the other

## GREAT GEEKY IDEAS

### Electronic Invitations

Whether you're inviting your family for a birthday celebration, the neighbors for a Fourth of July barbecue, or the girls from Bunco for an appetizer night, choosing electronic invites over written-and-mailed invitations can save you a bundle. Go to Evite.com, SignUpGenius.com, Pingg.com, Punchbowl.com, or Smilebox.com to look at free options for inviting guests via email, Facebook, or other social media. As much as I love the fact that electronic invites save me the cost of store-bought cards and stamps, what I love even more is being able to set up reminders for all my guests whenever I like.

with the most impressive super bargain twenty dollars ever bought. Clearance items, rummage sale finds, and a lot of goodwill and creativity keep this exchange a highlight of our holiday season.

# The Most Wonderful Time of the Year

For those of us who celebrate Christmas, it can be both the most wonderful, and the most stressful, time of the year. A big part of that stress comes from the seemingly never-ending expenses that come with fulfilling all the expectations of the season: gift giving, holiday décor, dress-up clothes, fancy feasts—it sometimes seems like peace on Earth won't be had until the Christmas season is behind us.

It can be stressful as a parent to not be able to have the holiday that you envision for your children, but a change in perception for the holidays can go a long way. Think of it this way: Your job as a mom, as a wife, as a daughter, and as a friend is to make the people you love feel special, and to help them create memories to carry with them. There is truly no set price (and no set time allotment, either) on that challenge. It's in the small choices you make, in the way you spend time with your family, and in the joy you share with them.

Here are some of my favorite ideas for making the Christmas season special, without spending yourself into trouble.

## DECK THE HALLS ON A DIME

For our first Christmas together, my husband and I spent a small fortune in a single preholiday shop—buying wreaths and ornaments, stockings, holiday plates, garlands, and ribbons—pretty much every trapping of the Christmas season that you can think of. I look back on it now and think how foolishly we spent that money. Yikes! Whether this is your first Christmas on your own budget or your fiftieth, you don't ever have to do it all at once. Think of holiday decorating as something you build on from year to year. Start with the basics, like a simple pre-lit tree. Then add something special every year: a wreath for your front door, a set of stockings for the mantel, a box of themed decorations that you fall in love with. Over the years, as you slowly build a collection of holiday decorations that have been hand-chosen (or hand-made) by you and your family, you'll come to appreciate the way each piece was carefully selected. Much of the stuff we bought that very first year on a one-store spree is gone now, broken or worn out or lost in the shuffle of our moves. The few "treasures" I have chosen each year since we started living on a smart budget, though, are here to stay. Each piece means something special to me, a part of a tradition we are carefully and slowly building together.

**Choose a "signature piece."** I'm a big fan of any cook having a signature dish or two to trot out for parties and get-togethers. I'm also a firm believer in a signature decoration for the holidays—rather than an avalanche of Christmas bric-a-brac that overwhelms your home. In my home, a pretty tree and a wreath on the door say all I want to say about our holidays: they are simple, cheerful, and beautiful—and frugal. I have a friend who has a collection of angels she displays every December; and another who trots out a box of beloved reindeer. One neighbor decorates her front porch with a gorgeous display of (fake) poinsettias, highlighted with a strand of twinkly white lights that winds among them. Each home has its own charm, and a distinctive style that says "this is *my* Christmas." If any of our homes had all of the above, they'd look overdone and ridiculous.

**Be a smart saver.** Don't be quick to toss away wrappings, ribbons, gift boxes, and the like after the holidays. Set aside a good-sized storage bin and save anything that might be helpful in future decorating, wrapping, or crafts. Ribbons and bows especially come in handy—and take up hardly any space in storage.

**Repurpose decorations year-round.** Who says a wreath has to be just for Christmas? Or a stocking holder, or even a decorative tree? Rather than spending a lot of time putting up and taking down decorations, consider redoing your displays for the next big occasion. A basic holiday wreath can easily be made into a great Mardi Gras highlight by using gold and purple ribbons, or a Valentine's Day welcome sign with red and white curlicues.

**Change your frame.** In our house, we have one large picture frame that's matted to an eight-by-eleven opening. In that frame, you never know what you might find. The beauty of a simple, prominent picture frame is that you can fill it with whatever strikes your fancy. Since the advent of Pinterest and other online "inspiration" boards, I have mile-long visual lists of the things that strike mine. For each holiday and special occasion, I change out the picture in this frame—sometimes a great picture of our family, sometimes a photo of a place I love, sometimes a cartoon or a saying or the lyrics of a song that I've printed from the Internet.

An ever-changing frame (or series of frames) can be used to display not only your favorite holiday images but also special mementos like a wedding photo during the week of your anniversary, a family picture from last year's barbecue for the Fourth of July, or baby pictures of each child on his or her birthday.

## MAKE A PLAN

To make the holidays more about traditions and less about fancy presents, help your family come up with a list of their favorite experiences of the season—and then help them live them. A great way to go about this is to create an "activity advent calendar" of December activities. On the first day of the month, sit down as a family with twenty-five small strips of paper, and write down lots of fun things you all want to do over the holidays. You might include one or more of these:

- Watch *Elf* at home and eat popcorn. After the movie, re-tell the story of Buddy's journey from the North Pole. Or choose another family-favorite holiday movie to enjoy together.

- Make a snowman. Dress him up and take pictures.

- Bake cookies and take a plate to your local firefighters.

- Make stocking stuffers for Dad.

- Draw a holiday picture and mail it to a relative.

- Make an ornament together.

- Attend your community's or church's tree-lighting ceremony.

- Read the true story of Christmas.

- Invite a friend over for hot cocoa and stir it with candy canes.

- Bundle up in pajamas and drive through the neighborhood to see the holiday lights.

- Build a gingerbread house (from a kit, unless you have a special talent for this!).

Once you've written down all the activities you're looking forward to, sit down with your calendar and fill an advent calendar (I make my own!) with the things you want to do on each day. As they open each activity, your kids will look forward to fulfilling this completely different kind of "wish list"—one that costs very little and that the whole family can enjoy together.

## KEEP A RECORD

One of the best ways to foster great memories for your children is to make sure they have plenty of mementos and photographs to look back on. Try keeping a family journal for the holidays. If you're clever and crafty, you can put together a wonderful scrapbook, but if you're a little tight on time and creativity, keeping a family journal like I do will fit the bill beautifully. I buy a simple journal, then put a copy of our family's outgoing Christmas card

### FAMILY TRADITION

#### Thoughtful Stockings

When our kids were very small, my husband and I decided to do something special with our Christmas stockings. Throughout the holiday season, I kept a pen and a pile of small paper squares on the kitchen counter. Every couple of days, the members of our family took turns writing special notes to one another. Ryan and I took dictation for the kids in the beginning (although they don't need our help anymore!). We kept the notes secret, not reading them as the kids put each one in the stocking of the person it was written for. On Christmas morning, in addition to finding a few goodies in our stockings, we each received a handful of notes, telling us how much we are loved, why we are special, and a few very sweet compliments about things like how we smell nice and how I make the best waffles in the world (!). Needless to say, reading those notes—and watching my family read theirs—was a highlight of my Christmas. We've been filling up thoughtful stockings for five years now, and I hope this treasured tradition is one that never ends.

(always a picture of all of us) in the front pocket. Our Christmas cards, letters to Santa, favorite recipes of the season, a list of fun things we did, and our favorite holiday photos go into this book each year. Even now, we love going through past years' books together and remembering "the good old days." As they grow older, I hope my children will treasure these simple records of their happy holidays.

## BRING THE CHEER

We all know that a big part of parenting is maintaining order and routine for our families. Plus, we've got to mind the rules, teach good manners, encourage good social skills, and so much more. That said, I think a good mom also needs to know how (and when) to let her hair down and just have some fun. Holidays, birthdays, and other special occasions are a perfect time to exercise your parenting creativity, encourage your kids to think outside the box, and even bend the occasional rule. Combining fun, out-of-the-ordinary experiences for your family can be a joyful, and often cost-free, way to make the most of special occasions. Here are some ideas my own family loves:

**Get loud.** One of the activities that always seems to end up on our holiday activity list is "take a bath with the Christmas carols blaring." I'm not sure how this one started, but it sure has held up well. The kids each get a big bubble bath, the holiday songs are turned up full blast, and everybody is just plain happy for a little while.

**Break a rule.** Have an eat-with-your-fingers meal. Jump on the bed. Have a gingerbread man for breakfast. Make an exception for a special occasion and watch your kids light up at the opportunity.

**Be silly.** What child doesn't love to see Mom and Dad let loose and be silly once in a while? (And what teenager doesn't dread it . . . ?) Game night has become a time when our kids know their dad and I are going to relax, giggle, and do the kinds of silly things required by a game of Twister, or Hedbanz, or charades.

**Wear your jammies.** The joy kids find in doing just about anything (except sleeping) in their pajamas is a mystery and a delight. One of our Christmas activities is get the kids all jammied up, hit up the Steak 'n Shake drive-through, then go looking at holiday lights in a nearby neighborhood. Just the idea of a take-out meal *and* an outdoor adventure in their pajamas sends my children into giggle fits. I know they're going to outgrow it one day, but I'm going to savor every season of this silliness while it lasts.

## FOCUS ON YOUR FAVORITES

We all know a mom who drives herself to the edge of a nervous breakdown over the holidays. It's so easy to let all the extra demands add up. Rather than trying to do everything, choose the things that really matter to you, and leave the rest to the Stepford wives. Here are a few suggestions for cutting corners to save yourself time and money:

**Keep meals simple.** Just because you're making Christmas dinner doesn't mean you really need to prepare two entrees, five sides, and multiple desserts. It's still just a meal, and the healthier, more sensible choice is to prepare one main dish, one or two sides, and a nice dessert. To make things festive, prepare an appetizer and set a pretty table. Make everything you can the day before, and spend the time you'll save enjoying the day with your family.

**Have a signature dish.** Whether you are going to an office party, a neighborhood get-together, or a Bunco gathering, have one or two dishes to bring that you can alternate. A great dip, a homemade cheese ball and crackers, a dessert your friends can't resist—whatever it is, keep the ingredients at the ready, and know your go-to recipes are ready any time you need them.

**Shop only when necessary.** Shopping, and shopping, and shopping some more during the holiday season can be a huge drain on both your energy and your finances. Always keep a running list of what you need. Don't make impromptu stops at the store. Plan your outings for efficiency and the fewest trips possible. I try not to go into stores more than one day a week—less if I can manage it. Not being overwhelmed by all the merchandise and the extras I don't really need saves me time and money.

**Shop online.** Not spending your time in the mall at all is even better than keeping shopping time to a minimum. If you don't need to browse, shop for decorations and gifts online. You can compare prices, get the best deal, and have your purchases shipped to your door.

# Ideas for Every Occasion

## BIRTHDAY CELEBRATIONS

Around here, everyone on our street knows when there's a birthday going on at our house, because we hang a birthday wreath on our front door. I'm not big on decorating for every occasion, but I do love to have one special thing that my family associates with each special event. Our birthday wreath is one designed by my much-admired fellow blogger at HowDoesShe.com, and I made it in about half an hour with less than fifteen dollars in supplies. Anyone can make one of these clever decorations with just a few packs of brightly colored balloons from the dollar store, a big package of greening pins, and a prefab straw wreath from any craft store. I use the pins to cover the wreath with balloons (not blown up!) and end up with a wonderfully festive, kid-favorite birthday decoration. In addition to choosing a simple, memorable, reusable birthday ornament, try these tips to make birthdays fun and keep them affordable:

**Alternate party and nonparty celebrations.** For children's birthdays, alternate activities. Having a birthday party is a rite of passage for a child, but I firmly believe that not every birthday has to have a big party to be a true celebration. Try alternating—one year a birthday party with your child's friends; one year a special family outing for the birthday, like a day at the zoo or the beach; one year a best-friend-only event, like a sleepover or mani-pedis and a movie together. Spreading the celebrations around will not only take the pressure off you to throw a big party every year but it will help your child appreciate lots of special ways to celebrate his or her big day.

**Choose the most frugal meal of the day.** If you're inviting a group of children for a party, try to schedule it in the mid-afternoon when you don't have to worry about a meal at all—just snacks and cake will do. If you're celebrating and need to include a meal, for example with your extended family, think about throwing a brunch or lunch instead of a dinner. A feast of breakfast casseroles, coffee, punch, and homemade cupcakes is one of the least expensive entertaining menus ever. Other reasonably priced meals for a crowd include a soup-and-sandwich menu, or simple backyard barbecue.

**Do a DIY dessert.** Bakeries be gone. Homemade cakes are hip. I have a book of cake recipes, complete with pictures, that is the holy grail of birthday preparation in our house. Not only are my children completely happy with a homemade cake, but they pore over the cake book for days before the big occasion, trying to decide which great recipe they'd like to have for their celebration.

**Choose thoughtful, but frugal, gifts.** With kids in school and lots of parties to be invited to, it's important to keep spending on gifts under control. My favorite gifts to give for kids' birthday parties are board games, card games, books (especially throwbacks to my own youth like Laura Ingalls Wilder and Beverly Cleary), outdoor activity items (like bubbles and sidewalk chalk), or arts-and-crafts supplies and kits. Many of these gifts can be picked up seasonally at huge discounts, and I make sure to keep a couple on hand at all times in case a last-minute invitation turns up.

**Write a letter.** For my son Ethan's sixth birthday, I wrote and framed a letter about all the things that had happened to him

# TAKE FIVE

## Five Great Kids' Birthday Parties on the Cheap

No matter what kind of birthday party you're throwing, keep in mind that the kids will remember laughing and having fun, not whether the cake was exactly round or the dishes were exactly matching. If you want to be a big hit with kids and their parents alike, make a point of taking a few great pictures of your guests that you can share in your child's thank-you notes.

- **Pretty-in-Pink Party.** When my beautiful Emily turned six, she invited five friends to spend an afternoon with us to celebrate. After her at-home party, she hugged me and told me hers had been the "best party ever"—music to my ears. The key ingredients of this fabulous soiree? Homemade pink cupcakes topped with Hello Kitty rings from the dollar store, homemade hot chocolate with marshmallows, tiaras (dollar store again), homemade tissue-paper pom-poms (pink, of course), nail polish with glitter, and a Barbie movie. Total cost: about forty dollars.

- **Princess and the Pea Party.** A wonderfully cute party for a little girl. Decorate with pairs of green balloons tied with pink ribbon. Make paper-and-glitter crowns for your little princess guests (or buy more tiaras from the dollar store). Three small round cakes with green icing make an adorable "sweet pea cake." Read and act out the story, and for a fun craft/guest gift, buy a multipack of white T-shirts and help your guests use craft paint to make "Give Peas a Chance" shirts to remember your party by.

- **Lego Party.** Build a party in your backyard by starting with a simple homemade Lego cake (a loaf pan–sized cake topped with marshmallows to resemble the nubs on a building piece, all frosted together). Baskets of Legos make fun party decorations, and free Lego printables for coloring help keep kiddos happy and busy. If you are a yard-sale shopper, keep an eye out for used Legos in advance of this event—these toys are 99 percent durable, and even though they're pricey new, you can often find them for a few dollars (or a few quarters!) secondhand.

■ **Baseball Party.** Decorate with red, white, and blue balloons or streamers. Serve ballpark hot dogs and buckets of popcorn. Make a plain, square cake something special by frosting it green and creating a baseball diamond on top with a brown frosting track and white frosted "bases." Or, make easy baseball cupcakes by frosting them white and then using red piping to make the "stitches" to make each one look like a ball. Play a small-scale baseball game in your yard or at the park (infield only so you don't need too many guests). If the weather isn't suitable, play Wii baseball or print (or make) free baseball bingo cards.

■ **Create a Cupcake Party.** This party is so fun and simple for small children (and for tweens and teens, who often don't want too much party structure, but can't resist doing a little cupcake art). Prebake a big batch of cupcakes, then provide all the "fixins" to make them birthday beautiful. An ideal mix could include prettily presented frosting, sprinkles, M&M's (separated by color if you want to go all out), small pieces of licorice, and gummy bears (or worms—whichever your child prefers!). The prettier you make the toppings seem, the more fun your little guests will have with this activity.

over the past year and how very special he is to us. We read it to him that night as his bedtime story. This gift meant so much not only to my son but to his dad and me, and to his grandparents, that I knew it would be the first of many. A special note, a treasure box with mementos from the year, a small photo album, or a framed letter are all great ways to show the people you love that they are treasured on their birthday.

## VALENTINES ON A DIME

While a part of me always looks upon Valentine's Day as a card-company holiday—as in they invented it so we would all spend money on it—I'm also a romantic. And so Valentine's Day has become a day when I try to find ways to show a little love without spending a lot of cash. Try these suggestions for a more heartfelt—and less costly—holiday:

**Write from the heart.** A homemade Valentine doesn't need to be sappy, but it can be full of the sentiments only you could share with your partner. Try writing a list of the top ten reasons why you love each other, or tuck a note in his lunchbox or under his pillow.

**Go to a little extra trouble.** Offer to give your Valentine a massage, or make a special meal, or create a romantic movie night. One of the Valentine's Days I loved most was a year that my husband and I couldn't get a babysitter for our son. We were broke and could not afford a dinner out, let alone the price of getting someone to babysit. That year, I borrowed a folding table and chairs and covered the table with a long tablecloth. I put a candle in the center and made us a steak dinner and bought a bottle of inexpensive wine. When my husband got home, I surprised him at the door and told him that I was able to get reservations at a great place and showed him our table. After our son went to bed, we had a wonderful dinner and conversation together. The food was superb and the price tag was just right.

**Print your own.** If you have children who exchange valentines at school, try choosing (or creating) a print-it-yourself card at home. There are tons of free printables on the Internet, and your child can personalize them if he or she wants to make them something special to share at school.

## ST. PATRICK'S DAY

Whether you're Irish or not, this is such a fun holiday to celebrate as a family! Who can resist the good cheer of this day of wearing of the green? If ever there was a holiday when the soundtrack made all the difference, this is the one. Put together a playlist of a handful of Irish standards ("When Irish Eyes Are Smiling," "McNamara's Band," "The Black Velvet Band," even "The Unicorn") and have a family sing-along. Use a little greasepaint to create shamrock "tattoos" for the day. Serve green milk with breakfast. And for a special treat, try making "rainbow in a jar" cakes—multicolored, festive-looking cakes to bring out the leprechaun in everyone in your family. Check out the recipes in chapter 3 for instructions.

## FAMILY TRADITION

### Earth Hour

One occasion that has come to hold a special place in our home is the commemoration of Earth Hour, an hour when individuals, whole cities, businesses, and landmarks turn off the lights to be mindful of our impact on the environment. The hour takes place from 8:30 to 9:30 p.m. on the last Saturday of March each year. It started as a local event in Australia, but by 2012 it was recognized around the world, and places as diverse as the Eiffel Tower, the Empire State Building, the Sydney Opera House, and our little house in Indiana were all participating.

In 2008, the first year it was recognized internationally, I read about this special hour and wanted to be a part of it. My husband and I decided to make it a special occasion we hoped our children would remember. The opportunity to stay up until 9:30 is special in and of itself for our kids, but staying up with the lights out was even more so. That first year, we let the kids take their baths by candlelight, then showed them how to make shadow characters on the wall. While they snuggled in their pajamas, we all talked about the energy we use, and about making sure we recycle and don't waste. Ethan especially loved our Earth Hour together, saying he wished every day could be that special.

What started as a simple chance to share a "moment" became an event to remember—and one we participate in each year.

## EASTER AND SPRING

Spring is the season when many of us moms get the special treat of dressing our kids up in their best for the Easter holiday and pictures. The problem is, it's easy to spend one hundred dollars or more on a child's new duds for the holiday—especially if you've got to buy shoes and hats and haircuts to go with the outfits.

**Save on special-occasion clothes.** Even if you're not typically a thrift-store shopper, when you're in the market for kids' dress-up clothes, perusing secondhand stores, Craigslist, or eBay can be a huge money saver. Most of the lovely dresses and boy-sized suits people buy for Easter Sunday, graduations, and other formal events only get worn one time, and then end up either given away, donated, or sold at a fraction of their original cost.

**More art supplies, less sugar!** When it comes time to fill Easter baskets, I'm a big fan of choosing a few inexpensive, useful gifts, rather than a bunch of sugar and chocolate! For small children, a new set of crayons, a coloring book, fruit snacks and graham cracker snacks can be a great substitute for candy or junk food (and you can get them all at the dollar store). Try to think of things that children of any age can use again or things that your child really needs (art supplies, beach toys, a fun indoor game, gardening supplies). Baskets like these will go a lot further than chocolate bunnies and marshmallow chicks.

**Make your own.** You can make your own Easter egg dye by mixing two teaspoons of brightly colored drink mix or food coloring with two teaspoons of vinegar. No need to invest in a prepackaged egg kit—this is easy-peasy to make yourself.

**Save it all.** Last, be sure you save your baskets, fillers, and empty eggs for next year's use. They are fine for use year after year.

## SUMMER FUN

**Make a plan.** Our family begins our summer planning with a big, giant list that we write together on poster board. On this list we write down everything we want to do over our summer with check boxes next to each item. The children decorate this list and then we hang it in our kitchen where everyone can see it. We add lots of low-cost activities we can do together like playing at the park, going to a lake, baking doughnuts together, running through the sprinklers, having an ice-cream-sundae night, planting a garden, and going to see a movie at the dollar theater. We are always excited to check these activities off our

---

### GREAT GEEKY IDEAS

#### Pinterest Summer Vacation Pinboard

Last summer, my family and I put a digital spin on our summer vacation board. With input from everyone, we created a Pinterest page with pictures representing activities for One Hundred Days of Summer. If you're not familiar with Pinterest, it's a free website where anyone can create a virtual pinboard for any topic that interests them. You can choose pictures from all over the Internet and "pin" them to your board, or you can upload your own photos and pin those. In the end, you get a wonderful visual collage of the things you've chosen. If you'd like to see a sample summer activity board, you can visit mine at pinterest.com/momadvice/100-days-of-summer.

list and it gives us something to look forward to all summer long.

**Explore your own backyard.** Each year we request a visitor guide to our own state and neighboring states. These guides offer a wealth of information about new spots in town and often are accompanied with coupons for area restaurants and hotels. Use these booklets as a guide for planning fun getaways in your own town and state, and explore them just as a tourist would. The booklets can highlight hidden gems that you may not have experienced yet.

**Get in touch with the great outdoors.** Summer vacation is the perfect time to get your family outside and in touch with Mother Nature. With extra time and extra sunshine, don't miss out on the chance to take advantage of all the wonderful (and free or cheap) activities that come with the season. Plant a small garden (or just a few flowers) with your kids, nurture them, and enjoy the beauty of watching them grow. Go pick berries and then make a homemade treat with them. Pack a picnic and spend the entire day at a park enjoying the changes as the day goes by. Create a small fire pit (if your neighborhood allows) and have a storytelling, s'mores-making night under the stars. Pitch a tent in the backyard and have a campout.

**Make some homemade fun.** Summer fun supplies can get costly very quickly. Rather than constantly buying your food and fun while you're on the go, plan ahead. Invest in a good small-sized cooler and make a habit of taking a snack and/or a lunch along with you when you go to the park, the pool, the library, or a friend's house for the day. You'll save a fortune in fast-food and quick-stop expense. At home, show your kids what a supermom you are by helping them make their own crafts and activities. Here are a few ideas:

## SUPER SIDEWALK PAINT

¼ cup cornstarch
¼ cup cold water
6 to 8 drops of food coloring

Mix cornstarch and cold water together in a small plastic bowl. Add food coloring and stir. Repeat this process to create different colors of paint. This simple paint can be easily washed away with water, so let your kids use it to their heart's content.

## TREASURE STONES

1 cup flour
1 cup used coffee grinds
½ cup salt
¼ cup sand
¾ cup water

Mix the dry ingredients together in a medium bowl. Slowly add water and knead until the mixture is the consistency of bread dough. Break off a piece of dough and roll it into the size of a baseball. Make a hole in the center of the ball big enough to hide "treasures" (a few coins, a special rock, a plastic dinosaur—whatever your kids want to hide). Fill the hole with treasures and seal with a little extra dough. Let your stone air-dry for two or three days or bake in the oven on a cookie sheet at 150 degrees for 15 to 20 minutes. If you would like to tint your stone, add 1 tablespoon of powder tempera paint to the mixture. Your children can break open their treasure stones if they want or hide them away with their secret contents!

## HALLOWEEN HAUNTINGS

Halloween strikes a fearful chord in a frugal mom's heart. Yet another holiday is here, one where mothers spend lots of money on one-use items—in this case costumes, worn once for just a few hours. Isn't it sad how much money we waste for such occasions? Here are a few ideas for avoiding the always-escalating expense of keeping up with the Draculas and princesses on the block:

**Swap with friends.** If you have a Bunco group, a book club, or a group of moms in your neighborhood who socialize together, suggest a costume swap a month or so before or after Halloween.

**Get retro.** Think back to your childhood and what costumes used to look like when we were children. Many of us were ghosts (made out of sheets), cowboys (wearing a cowboy hat and bandana), and ballerinas (a tutu and leotard). Most of our moms had a knack for using the resources they already had. The age of the Disney Store, costume catalogs, and a new manufactured costume for every kid, every year is a fairly new one. The fact is, many expensive costumes are ridiculously cheaply made and terrible-looking anyway, and you may very well be able to do better from your own closet and dresser drawers. Does your daughter love to play dress-up? Use one of her dress-up dresses and add a tiara. Instant princess! Does your son run around with a firefighter hat on? Add a rain jacket and boots and tell him he is a firefighter this year. Dress up a child in an apron, with a hairnet, a whisk and a cookbook to create the look of a chef. There are probably many items in your home that you can use in creative ways, without spending a dime.

**Get out the day after.** Shop after-Halloween sales, or call your local thrift store to see when they're going to put costumes out. Many of these shops pack away costumes all year long, then put them all on display in the early fall.

**Build your own.** Make something yourself. If you are crafty at all, a simple costume idea like an elf, a prisoner, or a clown may be well within your range of ability.

In addition to creating a simple costume, you can also make your own face paint. I can't even believe how expensive this stuff is when you buy it over the counter. A friend of mine spent sixteen dollars for two tubes of blue paint to outfit her son as a member of the Blue Man Group. You can easily make your own by mixing a tablespoon of cornstarch with a half tablespoon of cold cream. Once they are blended, add two teaspoons of water and your favorite color food coloring and you'll be ready to paint.

## THANKSGIVING FEASTS

Thanksgiving dinner is a job I've fine-tuned into manageability over the past few years. I won't bore you with the details, but I've learned to keep my menu simple, make any dish that allows it ahead of time, and not to sweat the small stuff. The essence of the day, though, has become something I try to live year-round, and something I try to teach my children, especially when Thanksgiving comes around.

One Thanksgiving-time project that can help any family get in touch with their inner gratitude is to create an album or slideshow of things they are grateful for, whether those are a job that pays the bills, a cozy home, a financial goal that's been met, a kind neighbor, family movie night, your smiling children, or just a great cup of coffee.

Another way to help your family visualize their good fortune is to create a Thanksgiving tree centerpiece. Take a few branches from the yard or park, spray paint them any color (or different colors), and arrange them in vase. Then make paper leaves in pretty fall yellows, reds, and greens. Set a stack of leaves beside your tree, and encourage everyone in your family to write down things they're thankful for on the leaves and hang them on the tree. It's a lovely way for kids to express themselves, and a chance for any family to stop and think about their blessings.

## AN OCCASION TO SHARE

It's important, on any budget, to stop and be thankful for the blessings in your life. And while it's something to be mindful of all the time, it's especially important when we are celebrating holidays, special occasions, and milestones in our lives. Sharing in your community is a meaningful way for a family to spend time together and mark any special occasion. By getting your children involved, you're teaching them to feel empathy and open their hearts to others, and you are also subtly reminding them how very fortunate they are. Participating in acts of kindness within the community sometimes has a fringe benefit at home, too: I can see my children exploring their kinder, gentler sides with one another and with my hubby and me as they do good deeds for others.

So many times we encounter the misconception that people who don't have a lot of money don't have anything to offer in charity. But anyone with a talent, a will, or an extra hour to spare can help someone in need. For example, at Christmastime our family takes board games and toiletry kits to the women's and children's shelter in our area. They are small contributions, but each one makes a difference and lets someone know we care about them. What better way to mark the holiday?

Here are a few suggestions for reaching out to others that will let your entire family experience the joy of sharing without breaking your budget:

**Use your talent.** Are you a baker, painter, knitter, teacher? Whatever your talent, there's a way to use it to benefit others. Think about volunteering in a school or a shelter, at a soup kitchen or at your church. Cook for a homebound neighbor, or walk dogs at the animal shelter. There are a million ways to reach out in your community and share your abilities. Personally, I volunteer to read with students who need a little help at a local school and I knit chemo caps and prayer shawls for our church outreach program—reading and knitting are things I love, so they're a perfect way for me to help others.

**Take a little time.** Every holiday season, my kids and I try to make time to bake cookies for our local firefighters. This has become a much-anticipated tradition for the kids, who both love to make something to tell these special members of our community that we appreciate them—and who also love the bonus of an adventure to the firehouse.

**Donate your change.** Do you have a spare change jar in your house that's gathering dust? Consider giving it to the Ronald

McDonald House Charities, where it will be put to good use helping provide shelter to families who have children in the hospital. A bit of change might not seem like it would make a difference, but this charity collected over twenty-five million dollars in contributions in 2010 alone—much of that in spare change.

## THE BEST MOMADVICE

### Be a Friend in Deed

One of the best examples I know of being able to make a difference in someone else's life without spending much (or even any) money is the relationship I have with an elderly gentleman I met one day at my local grocery store. He was studying the cuts of chicken, and asked me if I could explain the difference between the breast and the tenderloins. What might have been a thirty-second conversation turned into one that lasted a few minutes, as this nice man in his eighties explained to me that both his wife and his adult son had developed serious health problems, and so he was learning to cook for the first time in his life. He got a little choked up explaining his situation, but he was determined to rise to the challenge.

I have to admit that I was more than a little harried that day—racing through the market with a crabby three-year-old and the school's-out deadline looming. But I'm thankful that some better part of me let me take time to talk with this man and give him my phone number. I offered to help him anytime with cooking questions he might have. Since then, we talk and email from time to time, especially when Ed is making his grocery list, and my daughter and I have even been to his house so we can cook together. What began as an act of kindness has become a friendship for both of us.

# Gift Giving

Creative gift giving is a skill I've been honing since I was just a little girl. It began with homemade coupon books for hugs and chores and evolved into more grown-up giving with carefully selected thrift-store items and a knack for creativity in my kitchen. Having this flare for creative giving in my adult life gets me through the countless invitations to birthday parties, weddings, and baby showers that are sprinkled in with our daily mail. It seems that we're always celebrating an occasion in our house, and I wouldn't have it any other way, but being a thrifty and thoughtful gift giver lets us celebrate every occasion without breaking the bank.

Think of the gifts you've received in your life and what they have meant to you. The ones that stand out in my mind are not the most expensive, but are the thoughtful gestures from people who truly care about me.

I think back to my wedding day as we went through stacks of cards from our family wishing us well in our new life together. I do not remember much about the cards or how much money had been tucked inside them, but one card still stands out in my mind. My cousin had carefully hand-drawn a crossword puzzle in his card with funny clues, and my husband and I pored over that minutes longer than any of the other cards. I think of the poncho that my mother-in-law carefully knitted for me so that I could have privacy when nursing my newborn. I think of the delicious meals that welcomed me after the birth of our first child. I think of the babysitting that was offered for us as my husband and I wearily held hands at a dinner table, alone for the first time. Yes, these are the gifts that I think of, and those are the gifts I am sure you think of, too. These are the kinds of gifts I try to give, whether they're for a friend, a neighbor, a teacher, a pastor, or for a member of my family.

## CREATE A GIFT CENTER

You can have a gift closet, a gift drawer, a gift storage bin—whatever suits the space you have available at home. The purpose of a stocked gift area is twofold for your family. For one, you'll always be prepared no matter what occasion strikes. If you forgot to write something on your calendar or suddenly realize that your brother's birthday is looming and you have no funds for a gift, you can visit your closet and not stress. The second reason is to save your family money in this extra spending category. Why should you pay full price for a gift when you can seize a bargain opportunity when you see great gifts in the clearance sections and thrift stores? The important thing is to organize yourself for gift-giving occasions so you don't have to race out and buy a card and wrapping every time an invitation comes your way.

As you put together your gift closet, keep these few tips in mind:

**Give it again.** If you find a great gift at a great price for a child's birthday, a high school graduate, a couple getting married, or any special occasion, ask yourself if you might be able to use another. For example, I have a friend who stopped into a bookstore that was going out of business and found boxed sets of Curious George books and Judy Blume books at clearance prices. She bought the last three of each and stocked her gift closet for several lucky children with birthdays coming up.

**Have a signature style.** Personally, I love giving books, board games, and art supplies—all gifts that I think have nice longevity, since kids can come back to them again and again. For adults, I also like books, baked goods, and kitchen items, and creative baskets with themes like gardening, picnics, and winter warmth. Think about the things you treasure and see if there's a way to capture the essence of them in a favorite gift theme. Whether you're a traveler, a crafter, a cook, a decorator, or a supernanny at heart, choose gifts that are special from you, then personalize them for your recipients.

**Homemade is from the heart.** Last Christmas, I made fabric-covered button bracelets for some of the people on my holiday list. They are so pretty and worth every minute of effort, but it's hard to find a way to share just how special I hoped these would be. I wanted to write a note with each of them that said, "Handmade. Really handmade. As in, I broke my fingers a little bit. Because I love you that much." Fortunately, I didn't have to write that note to convey the loving sentiment behind the bracelets—my friends and family already know how much of myself I put into their homemade gifts.

Not everyone is a crafter, but if you happen to have a knack for knitting, stenciling, painting, sewing, making pottery—any talent at all, consider trying to use it as you make your gift-giving lists. We all know that time is at a premium these days, but so are friendships and family relationships. If there's a way to include a homemade item in your next gift, you'll succeed in being both frugal and heartfelt.

## GIFT IDEAS FOR EVERY OCCASION

### Graduation

I'm not a big fan of giving gift cards, but when it comes to new graduates, I make an exception. These are not the most inexpensive or clever present, but I know from experience that many a broke college kid truly, deeply, and honestly appreciates this simple offering. Choose a card for the grocery store, gas station, campus bookstore, or an inexpensive restaurant to make your new grad smile.

**College coupons.** My favorite thing to get in the mail when I was in college was a care package, so I often give coupons for care packages to the graduates in our lives. This very frugal gift has been a huge hit. To make it fun, create a menu-like checklist for your grad, complete with choices like homemade cookies, brownies, or other favorites that can be easily packaged and enjoyed. Assemble your order forms in a self-addressed, stamped envelope, and tell the grad you'll happily ship out a box of homemade goodies and affection whenever that envelope finds its way to your box.

**Life's little extras.** One great thing about giving to a grad is that they usually need everything, so you can't really go wrong: A laundry basket with a roll of quarters, a mesh laundry bag, detergent, fabric softener, and a Downy ball is a great idea; a shower tote with a towel, washcloths, and soaps; or (my favorite) a large dish tub neatly packed with "survival food" for the dorm, including plastic plates and utensils, ramen noodles, microwave popcorn, hard candies—in short, anything that can easily be prepared and eaten in a dorm room.

## Mother's Day

If you are a mom, you already know that the nicest gift for most of us is a day off from cooking. For Mother's Day and for birthday celebrations for the special women in your life, I highly recommend planning, preparing, and cleaning up a meal at which she is the guest of honor. Small extravagances like chocolate-dipped strawberries, a glass of champagne, a perfectly set table, and a beautifully plated meal make these occasions a chance to show a mom you are grateful for all she does and is.

## New Baby

Who doesn't love shopping for baby gifts? I'm not much of a shopper in general, but when I start looking at all those sweet tiny baby clothes and bibs and booties, the experience always makes me a little nostalgic and misty-eyed. When my children were babies, the gifts I appreciated most were the ones that gave me back a little time or sleep, two of the most precious commodities for any new mother. If you can give a new mom a smile or a moment of rest, you'll have come up with a gift that will be treasured.

**What's for dinner?** Meals for new mothers are a fabulous gift to give and cost next to nothing, except your time. I love taking meals to new moms because I remember how much I appreciated those meals when I received them—so often when dinner was otherwise going to be yet another scrambled egg or PB&J sandwich.

**Coupon for a mother's night out.** Paying for a babysitter is expensive, and finding a babysitter you can trust with a precious weeks- or months-old baby is a daunting challenge. A trusted friend and fellow mom who is willing to come to your home and take over so you can have an evening (or an afternoon) out is a great gift. Pair it with a bottle of wine and make that new mom smile.

**Personalized togs.** Onesies are a useful, practical shower gift, but you can easily "kick them up a notch" by personalizing them for the new baby. Use iron-on decals or fabric markers to customize onesies with the baby's name, initials, or an image that will make the new mom smile. You can even customize an iron-on with a home decal kit (available at office supply stores and superstores).

**A frugal first step.** If you're really stumped for a good gift, start the new baby off on the right foot with a charming piggy bank!

## Wedding

**Game on.** Start the happy couple's board game collection. I love the games that come in wooden, book-look boxes for a starter kit. They are inexpensive and fun, look great on the shelf, and can be a wonderful gift for a couple who are just starting a life together.

**Decorate their tree.** Holiday decorations can make lovely, special gifts for a newly married couple. You can purchase beautiful, cute, fun, and festive holiday décor at 75 percent off every year after Christmas—start a collection of ornaments that would make great gifts, and you'll be set the next time a wedding or housewarming comes around. To personalize this gift, add one ornament with the year of the wedding on it, and pack the gift in an ornament-organizing box that will last for years to come.

**A fine wine.** Fill a wine rack for the couple. I always keep an eye out for nice countertop-sized wine racks at thrift sales and garage sales. Since the rack is just the window-dressing for the wine, I'm always happy to find a used one is great condition in wood or wrought iron. I add a couple of bottles of a nice moderate-priced wine, a bottle opener, wine cork, and a pair of wineglasses to make a lovely, romantic gift for any couple.

**Dining alfresco.** Another great gift is a picnic basket paired with an outdoor blanket and a set of picnic utensils. These items inevitably end up on clearance at the end of summer every single year, and when I can snap one up for 70 percent off or so, I stock up my gift closet. This is always an appreciated, fun gift.

**An elegant note.** A stationery set can be a great gift for a new bride. Fill a basket with stationery, thank-you notes, quality pens, and a roll of stamps. This is a thoughtful gift that will undoubtedly come in handy when it comes time to write thank-you notes to shower and wedding guests.

## WRAPPING IT ALL UP

A beautifully wrapped package is a wonderful way to say "you are special to me" on any gift-giving occasion. Thankfully, anyone can learn to wrap with style without spending a mint. Skip the store wrap table and pare down your time in the gift-wrap aisle by using these tips to make your wrappings both frugal and fabulous:

- A deck of cards is great for making cute gift tags. Is your dad the prankster of the family? Give him the joker card! Does your mom rule over the whole family? Give her the queen. Wrap the whole family's holiday gifts with cards, and help them figure out who is who in the deck. Take a hole punch and loop the card through some ribbon, then attach it to your gift for a clever, original tag. Likewise, you can use old and unused board game pieces to jazz up gifts and personalize them. Things like loose Scrabble tiles and stray Monopoly pieces or Monopoly money make great additions to a clever wrap job.

• Wallpaper rolls are terrific resources for clever gift wrapping. You wouldn't believe how often leftover rolls end up being donated to thrift stores, and sell for just a few coins. The paper is very durable and comes in tons of smart-looking patterns and colors.

• When I make food gifts, I always make sure the packaging says "this is a nice gift" to go along with the heartfelt effort that goes inside. When I see seasonal tins on clearance at the dollar store or a thrift store, I stock up for any holiday— heaven knows they are all going to come around again! I also love customizing Ball jars, mugs, and plates for homemade goodies.

• Maps can be a clever way to wrap gifts. When you visit different cities and areas, pick up extra maps from the visitor center for gift-wrapping later. This is an especially great idea for souvenir gifts or for presents for a person you shared a trip with.

• I always keep a roll of inexpensive craft paper for my kids to use when creativity strikes, but we also put that roll to work when we need gift wrap for family members and for gifts from the children. They love personalizing the paper for their own gifts, and the "wrapping paper" they design is especially loved by aunts, uncles, and grandparents because it is made with love.

• I love making a gift look like something special by adding a decorative touch to the ribbon. I always have an eye out in dollar stores and thrift stores for objects that would be a nice complement to a themed gift or look nice on the wrapping. For example, mini-ornaments picked up from after-Christmas clearance sales look fantastic on next year's holiday gifts. Pacifiers and rattles make a baby gift something special. Housewarming and wedding gifts get a set of wooden spoons, measuring spoons, chopsticks—something fun that says "this gift was wrapped with care, just for you."

# 5

## Keep Your House Clean, Organized, and Welcoming

One of my favorite quotes is from British author and designer William Morris, who wrote, "Have nothing in your home that you do not know to be useful and believe to be beautiful." I put this philosophy in action every chance I get: rooting out clutter, displaying only objects I treasure, and keeping everything clean so I can appreciate the things I love. This philosophy has helped me learn not just to accept but to embrace our little house and take pride in its care and upkeep.

Unfortunately, being a good steward of your home can eat up a lot of time and money unless you've got a good system for keeping the work under control. My simple housework plan keeps our belongings in order, our furniture dusted, our laundry clean and put away, and my kitchen spotless (most of the time!). In addition to keeping our family's time spent cleaning to a minimum, I also keep our budget for this area small by making many of my own cleaning supplies. These simple product recipes are both green and effective—cleaners made from ingredients you know and trust, plus savings you can take to the bank.

## Keeping It All Clean and Organized

When it comes to cleaning and organizing my home, I take my inspiration from the highly competent, efficient, and frugal homemakers of old—not quite June Cleaver, but close! Most of our grandmothers used inexpensive supplies and cleaners made from a few household staples to keep their houses clean and looking nice. Rags made from worn-out clothes or cloth diapers, newspapers, and a basic mop and broom were the primary tools of the trade. In a day and age when cleaning caddies are crammed with chemicals that promise to be "scrub free" or even "magic," I kind of like the idea of using simple products and a little elbow grease to keep my home in good shape.

Having a clean, inviting home that says "welcome" to family members and guests alike is important to me. With a regular housework routine and a handful of homemade cleaning products, I feel like I can maintain that standard—at least most of the time.

### HAVE A HOUSEWORK PLAN

When I first got married, I had absolutely no clue on the basics of keeping house and how to maintain what we owned. Looking back, I ask myself how hard it really could have been to maintain our one-bedroom apartment with no children. It definitely seemed challenging at the time!

By dividing your housework into daily, weekly, and monthly chores, you can keep on top of the routine. The most important thing, I think, is just to start.

## Every Day

None of us—whether we stay at home, work nine to five, or juggle a part-time or work-at-home compromise—have time to waste. And if we did, we wouldn't want to spend it cleaning house. I'm a firm believer in investing a little time every morning to take care of as many housework basics as possible. Since I work from home, I can usually find thirty minutes each morning to work through my list. If you work full time, you may struggle to manage ten or fifteen. Any time you are able to invest in the morning, though, will give you the return of knowing a little order and cleanliness awaits in your home sweet home. Before the day starts to get away from me, I try to work through this list:

- Make bed.

- Wash breakfast dishes.

- Wipe down kitchen counters and sink.

- Do a speedy glass-cleaner-and-rag walkthrough of the bath-rooms, wiping off countertops and sinks.

- Start dinner. It may sound unusual to start dinner at 8 a.m., but I find that getting any prep work done first thing in the morning, along with the rest of my "put the house right" routine, sets up my day for smooth sailing. Any food prep (chopping vegetables, thawing meat, getting the slow cooker started) that can be completed in the morning saves time and trouble later in the day—when the after-school/ honey-I'm-home chaos starts to ramp up.

## Every Week

Once the morning jobs are complete, you can face the day with a good momentum going—after all, you've already got a clean kitchen, presentable bathrooms, and a made bed—oh, yeah, and your family will be fed! Whether you're settling in for a day with a houseful of kids or a full schedule at the office, you've already checked off a whole list of to-do essentials. The bigger tasks in my life are broken down daily into a system that has served me well over the years. Whether you work out of the home or not, having a plan to tackle certain areas of housework on certain days will keep you from neglecting important tasks and getting over-whelmed. Choosing a day for each job works for me to get everything accomplished and still have time to work and to enjoy my family.

- **Sunday:** Devote an hour or two on one day of the weekend (I choose Sunday afternoon) to get the house cleaned and organized. This will start your week off on the right foot. A quick vacuum and dust, a wipe-down of the bathrooms, a sweep of the front stoop—by the end of Sunday, I'm ready to take Monday morning by storm. As a freelancer, I also choose to do a lot of my work on the weekends. Saturday mornings and Sunday afternoons are getting-things-done times at my desk and on my computer. Starting my week with my blog posts written, my upcoming photos organized, my recipes chosen, and my house in order lets me be more of a full-time mom most days—a job I'm deeply grateful to be able to have.

- **Monday:** Around here, Monday is laundry day. With only four family members in our house, I am able to do laundry once a week, rather than multiple times like some of my friends. I know that laundry schedules may be different depending on your family size. The best part about tackling your laundry all in one day is that it helps your dryer to run more efficiently by running back-to-back loads, as well as giving you a chance to catch up on other jobs around the house, menu planning, or—on an especially good day—a hot cup of coffee and a good book during the inevitable waits for loads to finish. By the end of Monday, the clothes are all clean and put away, everybody's got clean sheets, and the house is still shipshape. If you work outside your home, combining laundry day and cleaning day may be the most efficient way to achieve order in your whole house in the least time. I have friends who choose to have a "house night" during the week—taking care of both laundry and housework on one weeknight so they can then have the weekend to rest, relax, and enjoy their families.

- **Tuesday:** Choosing to reserve one day for errands will help save on your gas expense, on time wasted in the shops, and on impulse shopping. For many nine-to-five workers, this day ends up being Saturday. For those of us who work at home and/or are stay-at-home moms, weekday errands definitely take less time. Tuesday is my day for accomplishing all of my shopping and appointments. I go out of my way to cluster my obligations on this day, so I don't spend any more time commuting and waiting than I absolutely have to. Make sure that you have your errands ordered in such a manner that you make the most of your time and your gas. This is my day for grocery shopping, banking, making returns, getting library books, doctor and dentist appointments, and volunteering at the school.

- **Wednesday:** Everyone has a pile of something that they dread doing. It could be paperwork that needs to be filed, setting up household maintenance tasks, or tackling that one room that becomes the family clutter catcher. As much as I hate it, I devote an hour every Wednesday morning to working on a task that has been pushed aside and neglected. Oftentimes, once I get started on the project, it seems I've fought half the battle—and that one hour can easily turn into two or three to get a job done and off my to-do list. No matter what your work or family schedule is like, finding your one hour for the put-off projects will give you a sense of control over your own personal chaos. Just the act of putting something on my list for this time each week (weed flower beds, organize pots and pans, wipe down baseboards) makes me feel like I'm halfway to accomplishing it.

- **Thursday:** We are blessed to have both sides of our family in town, and with lots of family comes lots of catching up, visiting, calling, and loving them. This is the day that I like to use for friend and family obligations, as well as my email inbox. This is also a great day to do something kind for someone else—an extra meal, an hour to lend a hand, or a gesture of kindness. Baking and testing out new recipes always fit well with Thursday's schedule. Even if you work full time and are just shaking your head at the thought of having time to bake on a Thursday, choosing to compartmentalize these kinds of visits, phone calls, letter writing, and sharing into one day will help keep all these seemingly small obligations from monopolizing your time and energy every day.

- **Friday and Saturday:** I enjoy having these days "off" to spend enjoying a homemade pizza with my kids, playing board games together, and catching up on my library reading. Even though I work on my blog and writing projects on Saturday mornings, it still feels like a restful day because I don't spend it racing from task to task or cleaning and organizing my home. I think setting my days up the way I do—front loading my work both each day and each week—leaves me plenty of time for truly enjoying our weekends.

## Every Month

Each month I tackle a heavy-duty cleaning project: things like cleaning the fridge; washing windows; reorganizing the cupboards; and going through each kid's room with a white glove, a garbage bag, and a donate box. Spreading the "spring cleaning" tasks throughout the year helps make them manageable.

## MAKE YOUR OWN CLEANING PRODUCTS

There's no downside to making your own cleaning supplies at home. They work as well as commercial brands, they cost much less, and they are healthier for your home and our environment than the harsh chemicals many commercial products contain. It's common knowledge that a healthy home is not doused in bleach and corrosive cleaners. I'd be lying if I said I don't sometimes turn to heavy-hitting chemicals to deal with industrial-strength grime, but I have long been learning to rely less on these cleaners and more on homemade versions. In addition, some basic household products can do double or triple duty for other uses around the house.

The main components of most homemade cleaners are white

vinegar, baking soda, liquid dish soap, and lemon juice. I buy vinegar and baking soda in bulk, and label clear spray bottles from the dollar store for my cleaning products. The savings on these homemade products can add up to hundreds of dollars a year. For example, a bottle of window cleaner usually costs you around three dollars. A bottle of homemade window cleaner will cost about five cents!

- **All-purpose cleaner.** Mix together two tablespoons of mild dishwashing soap (like Dawn or Palmolive) and two cups of water in a spray bottle and give it a shake. Use these anywhere that you would use a commercial all-purpose spray. This cleaner is particularly great for countertops, bathroom surfaces, and high chairs. This cleaner is also great for wiping down your plastic outdoor furniture to get it ready for the spring season.

- **Glass cleaner.** Mix together one part white vinegar to one part water in a spray bottle. Spray this solution on your mirrors and windows.

- **Scouring scrub.** Mix one cup borax, one cup baking soda (or you can use washing soda), and one-quarter cup salt. This can also be used in the dishwasher to clean your dishes (only one tablespoon is needed), and it can be a great scrubbing agent to add to your toilets, tub, and sinks to make them gleaming white again.

- **Oven cleaner/kitchen deep cleaner.** Mix a paste of three parts warm water to one part baking soda to clean away kitchen stains or to clean the oven.

- **Bathroom cleaner.** Mix dishwashing liquid with baking soda until you have a thick paste and use this throughout your bathroom.

- **Toilet bowl cleaner.** No measuring is required with this recipe. Sprinkle a little baking soda into your toilet bowl and then pour a little vinegar in and watch it fizz up. Give it a swish with a toilet brush and flush.

- **Tile and linoleum cleaner.** Add a half cup of vinegar to a gallon of water. The scent of the vinegar will fade in approximately an hour, but you can also add a couple of drops of essential oil if you want a particular scent. I like the smell of tea tree oil. Essential oils can be picked up at stores offering nutritional supplements or can be purchased online.

- **Furniture polish.** Mix a quarter cup olive oil with four tablespoons vinegar and two teaspoons lemon juice. Pour into a spray bottle and shake well before using. If you do not use all of it in one cleaning session, store the remainder in the fridge, as the lemon juice can go sour. You can also substitute the lemon juice with twenty to thirty drops of lemon essential oil and then you won't have to refrigerate it. Using the essential oils will up the price a bit on your homemade product.

- **Drain cleaner.** Pour a half cup of baking soda and a cup of vinegar down the drain, plugging the drain immediately until the foaming stops. Then rinse with hot water.

- **WD-40.** Sounds strange, but I always keep this handy in our house. WD-40 helps remove any sticky residue, and I use it constantly to remove crayon marks in our house (two-year-old plus crayons equals buying WD-40 in bulk!)

- **Newspaper.** Recycle your newspapers by using these to dry your mirrors and windows. They offer a lint-free solution and are a great alternative to other cloths, which can leave a dusty finish.

# TAKE FIVE

## Five Uses for Vinegar Around the House

Despite the fact that it can be worth its weight in gold to a homemaker, white vinegar costs about three dollars a gallon at Walmart—and even less if you buy it in bulk at a warehouse store. This one simple, inexpensive product is the housework equivalent of a miracle drug—cleaning practically anything and doing a great job. There are dozens of household uses for vinegar, but these are my favorite five:

- **Mom's little laundry secret.** You can spend a fortune on detergent boosters, stain removers, and fabric softeners, but you really can't beat plain old vinegar as a laundry aid. In the wash cycle: A cup of vinegar added will kill any lingering bacteria—an especially helpful function for parents using cloth diapers and for washing both new and secondhand clothes before wearing. Vinegar also works much like color-safe bleach, brightening whites and colors alike. In the rinse cycle: Half a cup of vinegar will help get all the soap out, soften your clothes, remove static, and deodorize. If you have hand-washing, two tablespoons of vinegar in your sink rinse will do the same job on a smaller scale. Prewash: If your clothes (or your children's clothes) are faded from multiple washings, soak for an hour in a mixture of one cup vinegar in a gallon of water to brighten. For coffee, tea, wine, ketchup, or grass stains, soak the stain in a mixture of one-third cup vinegar, two-thirds cup water, line dry in the sun, then wash as usual.

- **Clean-up-quick tool.** Use a cloth dabbed in vinegar to clean and polish chrome and stainless steel. This works great for getting greasy fingerprints off stainless appliances. Use the

same method to remove mineral stains from nonstick cook-
ware, scissors, and silverware. To loosen up baked-on gunk in
your glass bakeware, fill the dish with a half cup vinegar and
hot water and let soak.

- **Super odor reducer.** Boil a tablespoon of vinegar in a
couple of cups of water to remove the odor of last night's dinner from your kitchen. Set out a bowl half full of vinegar to soak
up odors in any room of the house. For a quick refresher, keep
a spray bottle containing a tablespoon of vinegar diluted in a
pint of water; spritz areas that need odors removed.

- **Fight frost.** To prevent frost from forming on your car's
windshield on frigid nights, spritz it with a mixture of half vinegar, half water before dark.

- **Microwave magic.** To help remove sticky stains and splat-
ters in the microwave, heat a glass bowl containing a half cup
vinegar mixed with a cup of water for four minutes on High.
Leave the microwave closed and let the vinegar steam for ten
minutes, then use a sponge to easily wipe the interior clean.

## Simple, Frugal, Stylish

Home décor is a spending category I've never had much budget
for. I love a Pottery Barn catalog as much as the next girl, but you'd
never catch me spending three hundred dollars on a wall mirror,
or one hundred dollars on a handful of silk plants. I'm just too
frugal for that! Fortunately, appealing and tasteful style does not
have to be expensive. By working with what you have, finding
inspiration for creative ways to create looks you love, and empha-

sizing the things that make your family special, you can have a home as beautiful and cozy as anyone's catalog—on any budget.

## STEERING CLEAR OF CLUTTER

Clutter is the great décor buster of even the most beautiful home. It's also a huge budget buster—requiring you to constantly be rooting around for things you want and need, getting in the way of productivity, stressing you out. Plus, it would seem you bought all that stuff to begin with and it has surely turned out to be a waste of money. Clutter is a big side effect of our consumerist society, and with every passing year I become more aware of how much more I love a spare, clean-looking room (or desk, or closet) than one that is filled to the brim with things I don't truly want or need.

Keeping clutter at bay is something I try to be mindful of every day, but once a year, our home undergoes a "Cut the Clutter Challenge." The end result of this thirty-day adventure is feeling like I haven't just cleansed some of the materialism from my home but from my very soul. To get this wonderful feeling in your home, follow these clutter-cutting guidelines:

**Start small . . . really small.** When you survey your house as a whole needing to be de-cluttered, it's easy to feel defeated. Jotting "organize the house" at the bottom of your To Do list does not seem like a feasible goal—it seems like a bit of a cruel joke. Instead, choose your month to clear out your clutter, and start with one small spot in your home on your task list. Choose a place that's been bothering you, so you'll want to get started! It could be as small as the kid's bath toys, a junk drawer that could give under its weight of uselessness, or simply a single shelf in your home office. I found that once I began a junk drawer, for example, I would then start moving into the drawer below it, and then the next. Building the momentum to tackle a whole mountain of clutter in your home starts with achieving success in a couple of small spots.

**You don't need another basket.** I remember when I first began organizing my home, I thought it was all about buying organizers, storage containers, and pretty baskets to give all my belongings a "home." Alas, all that effort got me was a house brimming with baskets of items I didn't need or never used. Instead of thinking of how to make the items you have more attractive and accessible, consider if you really need the items themselves. If you don't really and truly love or use them, get rid of them!

**Set aside sentimentality and regret.** Two things get in the way of me letting the items go in my home: sentimental feelings about my "special" clutter, and that woeful "but this was so expensive" feeling that comes from chucking something you spent too much on. The things I struggle most with are often gifts and items that were special to my children when they were small. I must admit that as adamant as I am about de-cluttering, these two feelings are capable of stopping me in my tracks. If you run into this problem, try this compromise: give yourself a large plastic tote (or two) in the basement or attic where you can save mementos you can't quite part with. Over time, one of two things will happen: your attachment may start wearing off, or you may decide these things must stay. Either way, you've got them out from underfoot while you take the time to decide.

**Get back to square one.** My last Cut the Clutter Challenge yielded fifteen garbage bags and three large totes of uselessness from our lives—and did I mention I do this once a year? Once you've gone to all the trouble of getting your house in order and clutter-free, I know you'll be more mindful of what you bring home to add to your environment. To keep clutter from creeping back into your life:

- If you see something you want, ask yourself, "Do I love it? Do I need it?" If you're not sure, wait a day before buying.

- Ask for gifts that are experiences, not things. When you make your birthday wish list, or help your children with one, why not ask for movie passes? Or ice-cream-shop gift cards? Or the cost of a class you've always wanted to take?

- Learn to subscribe to the "something comes, something goes" rule. If you bring home a new object, try to donate or dispose of one to balance it out. In this way, you can keep clutter from mucking up your home, interfering with your peace of mind, and constantly adding to your budget's bottom line.

## THE BEST MOMADVICE

### Personalizing Your Art

When we decorated our first home, I thought that all of the artwork should be purchased at a department store, chosen in carefully selected colors that matched our home. Weren't we all taught this? It had never occurred to me until more recently that everything in our home, including our artwork, could be personal to our family.

One of my favorite walls in our front room is decorated with three simple frames with three black-and-white pictures of shoes. The first picture is of my daughter's tiny foot dangling as she was swinging in the air at the park. Her little lacy socks and Mary Jane shoes were too perfect not to photograph. That shoe choice spoke volumes about Emily's girly-girl attitude, even for a day of playing in the mulch. The second picture is a shot I took in the fall, my favorite season, of my entryway with all of the pretty fallen leaves and pretty pumpkins on our front step. My favorite fall boots are resting in the corner after I had come in from a day of raking. The last picture was my most glamorous day ever—a photo shoot in my home with *Redbook* magazine, when our family had been featured for living a life without credit cards. My shoe is touching the taped "X" that the photographer had placed on our carpet to mark my spot for the picture. It was one of the most fun and exciting days for our family, and that moment sealed the deal on our credit card–free life. The cost for this personalized artwork? Less than five dollars for these beautiful prints, and they make me happy every time I gaze at them.

Over the years, we have added other photographs to our home as our art. The year my daughter was Dorothy from *The Wizard of Oz* for Halloween yielded a beautiful photo of those infamous ruby slippers with fallen leaves surrounding her tiny feet. Our family Christmas card was too beautiful to put away in a box so I placed it on a corner table in our family room so I can appreciate it all year long. Quotes from Audrey Hepburn with strong words about how to be a truly beautiful girl hang on my daughter's wall, purchased for a small price on Etsy, hung in dollar-store frames I spray painted to match the décor in her room. As you can see, the possibilities for personalization are endless and often inexpensive.

## IDEAS FOR EVERY ROOM IN THE HOUSE

Finding ways to feature the things you love will help make your house into a home full of personal touches. "Things you love" can be anything, by the way, not just framed art or traditional knick-knacks. Here are a few ideas to make any room feel warm and inviting for your family and your guests—every concept for low cost or no cost. For about a million more ideas, check out Pinterest.com, where you can create a virtual pinboard of ideas you love to revisit anytime for inspiration:

### Entry and Living Areas

**Themed photos.** Anyone can make a photo display using just your own photography and inexpensive frames from rummage sales, thrift stores, the dollar store—it doesn't matter where you get 'em. If you have a series of frames that don't go together, haul the whole batch out in the yard and spray paint them the same color. Voilà—you have a matching set.

Don't be afraid to experiment with different photo finishes; colors that "pop," black-and-white, or sepia tones can all be beautiful. If you order your prints online, you can experiment by trying out all kinds of photo effects before settling on your favorite. Waiting a couple of days will save you half price or more on the cost of one-hour printing, too.

Some of the nicest photo collections I've seen are of family members on the beach at different ages and stages, baby pictures with Mom and Dad, and an assembly of wedding pictures of parents, grandparents, and great-grandparents. Vary the sizes and focal points of your photos to create an eye-catching display that beats the pants off those school-picture collages everyone seemed to have on the wall when I was a kid.

## YOU DO THE MATH

### Photo Gallery Wall

Ten picture frames from a high-end home design store, matted to 8 by 11 and 5 by 7, all matching: minimum $280 (on sale)

Ten picture frames from Target, Walmart, and the dollar store, spray painted to match for my display: $46

Savings: at least $234

**Mementos from places you love.** In our home, we have a poster with the names of many different cities in black and white, with Boston, where we started our married life, highlighted in red. I have a friend who made one of these herself at the kitchen table with easy stencils and paint. Little tributes to the places you treasure can give your home a feeling of shared history and adventure. Rather than piling up bric-a-brac on your surfaces, though, look for souvenirs that are suitable for frames and shadow boxes—a black-and-white sketch from a street vendor, a photo of you in front of a favorite place in your hometown, a map of a historic area—putting a few elements together, you can create a fun display that costs nothing more than the time spent rummaging around for your favorite souvenirs.

## Kitchen

**A few of your favorite things.** If you've visited me at MomAdvice.com, you might have noticed I have a thing for aprons! Everything about them seems charming to me. So having a place to display them is a natural fit for my kitchen. A row of uniformly separated hooks provides a perfect place to hang my favorites—and gives the kitchen a warm, personal vibe. If you have a favorite kitchen item, don't hide it away in a cupboard. Give it a place of honor—somewhere other than on your countertop, since we don't want to start cluttering that up. Do you have a couple of pretty copper pots that are well loved but seldom used? Hang them instead of artwork on your kitchen wall. Antique kitchen utensils from garage sales or thrift stores also make creative, eye-catching displays. If you have treasured, stained, and well-loved family recipes on cards or notepaper, framing and hanging them will not only preserve the handwritten versions but make a charming, personal decoration for just the cost of the frames.

## Master Bedroom

**"Love me do" wall.** One of my favorite displays in our house is a little tribute to my partnership with my husband in our bedroom. I dusted off some of the old relics in our basement, including the Post-it note I gave him with my name and number the night we met in high school, the keys to my heart I gave him when we were dating (cheesy, I know!), and a wonderful picture a friend of mine took of us together. Using simple matte black picture frames and a shadow box, I arranged them all on one wall in our bedroom. You could use anything that's special to you and your partner to make this kind of display—a room key card from your honeymoon, ticket stubs or a menu from a special night out, or a note that came attached to a bouquet of flowers would all be great. To up the nostalgia factor, top it off with a sweet hanging sign, like one of the ones that say "Always kiss me good night" or "And they lived happily ever after." Just looking at this wall at the end of a hectic day reminds me how lucky I am and helps melt my stress away.

## Kids' Rooms and Playrooms

**A reader's room.** Years ago I saw an article in *Real Simple* magazine that featured kids' room artwork created from book jackets. This was such a wonderful idea, I tackled the project right away. A trip to the dollar store and a quick shuffle through the bookshelf yielded dollar frames and the jackets from a few of my son's favorites, including *How Do Dinosaurs Eat Their Food?* and *How Do Dinosaurs Say Good Night?* The result was a kid-friendly, reader-friendly, dinosaur-loving room—this is a wonderful, almost-free idea for any child with favorite book characters.

**Starring the artist.** Of course, you can't go wrong using your children's own artwork to decorate their rooms. Framing and hanging your child's hand-print pictures and stick-figure family drawings will make him or her smile; or you can create an ever-changing display by stringing a length of clothesline along one wall and providing colorful clothespins for each new masterpiece.

**The story of my life.** Kids love nothing more than to see and hear their own stories. Let your child help you create a wall with a storybook theme about him or her. You can start with a baby picture, and use either a caption on the photo mat or stencils to begin the story, such as "Once upon a time there was a prince . . ." As you add each photo, add a story line (for example, caption a photo with the family dog "and his furry beast was named Rover," or a vacation pic with "he traveled far and wide"). Let your child help you choose the pieces of his or her story to tell—and always leave a little room for the next adventure. For the cost of a few framed photographs and a little of your time, you can create a tidy, but beautiful and personal, display.

## LIVING WITH LESS AND LOVING IT

Small-space living comes with many challenges, but the rewards for a family on a budget are great. For a long time I considered our smaller home a temporary place to get us by until we could afford more. As the years have gone by, though, I've discovered the power of living in a smaller house and making the most of what we have been given.

Small space is all relative, of course, isn't it? In full disclosure, our home is fifteen hundred square feet for our family of four. Regardless of your square footage, I wanted to share a few ideas for learning to embrace the space you're in right now:

**Furnish right.** Furniture can make a room feel larger or smaller depending on its size, placement, and purpose. Large furniture we purchased for our previous home was not well suited for the home we have now, but replacing it was a cost that we couldn't afford. Rather than go shopping for new pieces, we scaled back, using less furniture in each room. If you have a room that's looking overstuffed, ask yourself which items are really being used. Are those side tables serving any function? Is the coffee table really needed or would your space benefit from an ottoman that could also serve as storage? Is your extra seating frequently occupied, or is it just taking up space? Try removing pieces of furniture from the room and see if they make the flow of the space feel bigger.

When you do replace furniture, try buying items that could serve dual purposes or could maximize your smaller rooms. When my son needed a new bed, we opted for a loft bed that would allow him to have a desk underneath: one piece of furniture that he would truly need and one that would not have fit with any other piece.

**Cut the clutter by half.** The best part about living in a smaller space is that it forced me to edit the belongings I have and has kept me from buying as much as I would in a larger space. If your home closets are small, if you don't have a basement, if there is no garage . . . well, then you have all the more inspiration to keep clutter under control.

**Repurpose spaces that aren't working for you.** Look around your home and ask yourself if there is any space going to waste. A closet full of clutter that no one ever opens? A seldom-used guest room? A dining room where your family doesn't dine?

These spaces have great potential to become useful, enjoyable spaces with a little creativity and an idea for how they'd better work for you. Look through a few home décor magazines or catalogs for inspiration. Some closets are easily converted into hideaway home offices. A guest room with a futon rather than a bed can become a playroom for children, or a workout room for Mom and Dad. Your dining room might serve your family much better if you use it as a game room (with shelves for your board games and a table permanently set for checkers or chess) or a family library (with a homework table, a shelf for books, and maybe a comfy reading chair). Try to think of ways your unused spaces can work with your family's lifestyle and needs.

**Make your space feel permanent.** If you're thinking of your home as a temporary place until you find something bigger or better, you might be overlooking the chance to really make the space you're in work for your family. When I finally told myself that our little house is in fact my long-term home and put some creativity and elbow grease into it, it transformed not only the space but my attitude. I look around now and I don't see a little house that wasn't what we wanted. I see the home my husband and I are happy in, the place we are raising our beautiful children, the setting of some of the best memories of my life. Our little home has become a place I truly love.

## Everything for Your Home, for Less

When I was a little girl, I loved playing house. As an adult, it still makes me happy to look around our home and know that everything is the way I arranged it, that this is my family's place, full of memories and good things to come. But there's a whole other side to grown-up housekeeping—the side that takes up tons of time and costs a small fortune. Expert recommendations for annual home-maintenance costs range from 1.5 to 4 percent of the home's original cost. If you happen to have bought a lemon or an older home, you could easily be looking at well over that 4 percent cap. Ryan and I got a killer deal on our 1960s split-level house, but within the first few years of owning it, we had to replace our air conditioner, furnace, windows, and front door. There may be no avoiding extra expenses when you own and maintain a home, but there are plenty of good ideas for keeping things shipshape and looking nice at the lowest possible price.

## GETTING THE MOST FOR YOUR MONEY

There are certain costs of home ownership that simply can't be avoided—like when a major appliance goes belly up or the roof starts to leak. Most of the costs of decorating, maintaining, and repairing your home, though, can be reduced through careful shopping, creative thinking, and a little (or a lot) of elbow grease.

### Frugal Furniture Finds

Furnishing your home can be both a privilege and a burden— you can make it any style you like, *but* you've got to pay for it. Try these tips to get the most for every dime of your furniture spending:

**Choose a classic style.** When choosing major pieces of furniture for any room, always err on the side of a simple, classic style. There are a million ways to personalize, update, or restyle any room by tweaking and changing the details, but a big, style-specific piece of furniture won't want to cooperate when you want to make a change. Try to choose pieces with clean, simple lines, durable fabrics, solid construction, and when you can, materials like hardwood that will hold up to staining, painting, and refinishing if you choose.

So I know what you're thinking: sounds like this is a shopping list for a high-end furniture store—and frankly a girl could drop more on one sofa than most of us have for a whole room (or whole house) budget. The thing to remember, though, is that good furniture will last anywhere from a couple of decades to, well, forever. So why bother with buying it new? Even though I love a good IKEA bargain as much as the next homemaker, my best furniture bargains have come from shopping my local classifieds, Craigslist.org, yard sales, and secondhand furnishing stores. These sources offer an ever-changing array of great (and not-so-great) furniture for sale at prices that are usually a small fraction of the cost of new goods.

**Keep an open mind.** In our house, my favorite piece of furniture is a desk that I got for about eighty dollars after finding it on Craigslist. It was oak and a little ugly, with a finish that went with nothing whatsoever in my house. But it was hardwood, solidly made, and something about it just spoke to me. I brought it home, much to my husband's dismay, and made it my pet project for a few days. After a quick sanding, I painted my new desk a soft matte black. I couldn't help but notice how much better it looked without its old brass hardware, so I spray painted the knobs and pulls with a brushed silver spray paint before replacing them. I repurposed the whole piece as a china

## GREAT GEEKY IDEAS

### Check Out Freecycle.Org

Have you been to Freecycle yet? The Freecycle network is a nonprofit website that was created to help keep durable goods out of landfills. What started as a local project in Tucson, Arizona, has become an international marketplace for people who have stuff to give away and people looking for something for free. Nearly nine million people are members of this green movement. You have to be a member to participate, but membership is free, and everything listed here is free. If you are trying to find something specific—say, a twin bed frame—you can create a "wanted" ad to help you match up with someone who has one to share.

cabinet, and today it is a focal point of our dining area—a great combination of classic and kitsch that I love.

**Know the good stuff when you see it.** When you buy used furniture, look for any telltale signs it's not going to hold up. Sagging cushions and fraying fabrics are a no-no, unless you've got some sewing and refurbishing skills. Wood joints that are attached by means of pegs or staples aren't likely to stay together for long. If you find a piece of wood furniture with tongue-and-groove construction in the drawers or joints, know you've probably got a restorable, quality piece on your hands. If you don't know much of anything about furniture repair, consider trading favors with someone who does to get them to come with you on a scavenging day. Offer a great home-cooked dinner, a special cake, typing or editing services—whatever you've got—to have someone along who can tell you what kinds of furniture quirks are easy to fix and which ones are fatal flaws.

## TAKE FIVE

### Five Simple Home Repairs You Can Handle Yourself

Thank goodness for YouTube! Whenever I have a task I think I might want to try to do myself, I watch a few how-to videos before I decide. Qualified people in almost any field you can imagine post their videos and step-by-step instructions. Don't get me wrong—I believe anything you find on the Internet needs to be taken with a grain of salt—but, watching an instructional video usually gives me a pretty good idea whether Ryan and I are going to roll up our sleeves and figure something out—or get on the phone for a repairman.

These jobs are often hired out, but we've found they are all simple and straightforward to do on your own.

■ Replace filters for electric heating/air-conditioning. This job that people often pay a service person to do for them is easy-peasy to do yourself. Check your unit or its manual to see which filter you need to order, then follow the easy steps on the manufacturer's website to do the installation yourself.

■ Lawn care and landscaping. I know so many people who pay someone to mow their lawn or to rake their leaves or put in seasonal flowers. Maybe it's because I spend much of my work time sitting indoors, in a chair, with my eyes on a computer screen, but these outdoor jobs are something I not only choose to do—I'm happy to do them. Doing your own yard work can save one hundred dollars a month or more.

■ Weatherproof. If you live in a cold climate, caulking around windows in the winter can save you a bundle on your heating bill.

■ Unclog the toilet. I know, yuck. However, I actually have friends who will call a plumber just for a clogged commode. Buy yourself a plunger for five dollars and learn to use it. You probably won't need a YouTube video for that one!

■ Fix a sticky lock. You may not have to call a locksmith to get a stubborn lock undone. If you have a lock that doesn't want to turn, pick up a small tube of powdered graphite at the hardware store (if you have a Boy Scout who makes pinewood derby cars, you probably already have one around the house, since this is what they use to make the wheels turn faster). Squeeze a little graphite into the keyhole, then insert the key and use it to distribute the graphite around the lock. More often than not, this will solve the problem.

## Hiring a Contractor

If you have to have a roof done, a bathroom updated, a room re-done, or anything else that requires skilled labor, you've entered a murky world where all too many people end up paying more than they have to, struggling to get the job done right, and even winding up with shoddy work. To get the best workers and the most with your money, always get multiple bids for any job. The more, the better. In a friendly but professional manner, make it clear up front that you have a limited budget, that you will check and double-check every invoice against the work, and that you will need (and check) references.

Once you've got your bids, keep an open mind. Most of us jump to the conclusion that the lowest bid will represent the shoddiest work and the highest will represent the best—neither is necessarily true. One contractor may need the job more than another, may be more efficient, or may have other legitimate means of keeping costs down. Rather than jumping to any conclusions, double- and triple-check the bids to make sure all the materials and methods are the same. Then start calling those references. If you can find three strong recommendations for recent work, you're probably in good shape with your best-price contractor.

Before you seal the deal on a contract, negotiate payment terms. Be very wary of anyone who insists on a big portion of the total up front. A fair deal would be 10 percent down and then three or four equal payments as the job progresses. Make sure there is one payment reserved for the very end—when you are happy with every last detail of the work.

# FRUGALLY EVER AFTER

When I started writing MomAdvice nearly ten years ago, I was so eager to learn how to stretch a paycheck, how to make the most of my resources, and most of all, how to live frugally without feeling like my life—and my family's— was all about "doing without." Every day that I learned a way to better accomplish those goals, I put it on my blog. At the time, the economy was strong, Facebook and Twitter were yet to take root, blogs and books hardly knew one another, and I often felt like I was shouting my message of frugality through a very tiny megaphone to an incredibly small niche community. Sometimes I wondered if I was just talking to myself!

Over the years, I've learned a million things and tried to write about them all—how to feed a family of four on almost any budget; how to say no to pricey gadgets when so many moms are saying yes; how to turn a simple Sunday morning breakfast into a "wafflepalooza" my kids greet with delight; how to create a summer vacation full of laughter, sunshine, and great memories without even stretching—let alone breaking—the budget. In short, I've helped my family find a way to truly enjoy the good life for less.

Through our journey, I've been reminded just how much I already have to be grateful for. No matter where we were financially, taking one look at my family made me realize just how much we were blessed. As author Jacqueline Winspear said, "Grace isn't a little prayer you chant before receiving a meal. It's a way to live." Living frugally has made me so much more aware of our family's every blessing, great and small. It's a richness that money can't buy.

I hope this book will help you find your own path to living frugally and well, and to enjoying the peace of mind and many blessings that can be created by living a more simple life. Many thanks for sharing in our journey and for taking the time to read some of my favorite MomAdvice.

# ACKNOWLEDGMENTS

I would like to begin by thanking Jana Murphy for helping me bring the vision for this book to life. Our endless hours chatting on the phone about the chapters and our emails never felt like work to me. I am so happy to have found a great friend in you and to have your partnership on this project. Enormous thanks goes to Erin Niumata, my amazing literary agent, for believing in me and my family's story and never giving up on this book. Your conviction empowered me and made this dream a reality. I am thankful to Jeanette Shaw, my editor, for the devotion and time she put into editing this book and shaping it into what it is today. I am also so thankful to the entire team at Penguin for their efforts and for their clear and perfect vision for what this book should be. For the beautiful cover photo, I'd like to thank Nancy Lary Studios, Gabrielle Thompson, Jesica Keller, and Andrea Weiss. I felt like the luckiest girl in the world that day to have such a great team behind me.

Thank you to my parents, siblings, and in-laws for their endless encouragement to pursue my dream. With gratitude in my heart, I thank Becky Kintzele for being my rock through this entire process. I could not ask for a better friend. Thank you to my children for always being my greatest inspiration—without the two of you, this project would never have happened. Most of all, I thank my husband for being the best thing that's ever happened in my life. Even when we had nothing, I had everything.

# INDEX

# ABOUT THE AUTHOR

**Amy Allen Clark** has been the driving force behind MomAdvice .com since its inception in 2004. In addition to running a successful community for women and running after her kids, she has served as a spokesperson for Minute Maid, Cascade, Glade, ALDI, and Cheer and is currently a spokesperson for Kenmore. Amy is also a contributing writer for Walmart, Snackpicks, and Goodwill. She resides in Granger, Indiana, with her husband and two children.